IN
PRAISE
OF
PLODDERS!

IN PRAISE OF PLODDERS!

... AND OTHER MINI-MESSAGES OF ENCOURAGEMENT TO THOSE WHO MINISTER

WARREN W. WIERSBE

In Praise of Plodders
© 1991 by Warren W. Wiersbe

Published by Kregel Publications, a division of Kregel Inc., 2450 Oak Industrial Dr. NE, Grand Rapids, MI 49505.

Illustrations: Les Remmers

Library of Congress Cataloging-in-Publication Data
Wiersbe, Warren W., 1929–2019.
  In praise of plodders / Warren W. Wiersbe.
  p. cm.
Includes bibliographical references.
  1. Clergy—office. 2. Clergy—Religious life. 1. Title

BV660.2W47   1991   253.2—dc20   91-10911
                               CIP

ISBN 978-0-8254-4841-6

Contents

Preface

T he essays in this book were originally written for *Prokopē*, a bimonthly newsletter for Christian workers published by Back to the Bible, Lincoln, Nebraska. I want to thank Back to the Bible for allowing me to reprint a selection of them here.

Prokopē (pronounced PROK-uh-pay) is a Greek word that Paul used in 1 Timothy 4:15. The Authorized Version translates it "profiting," while the NIV and NASB use "progress." It means "pioneer advance" and comes from a verb that means "to cut forward." The purpose of *Prokopē* is to challenge the minister to grow intellectually and spiritually and to move courageously into new experiences of growth and service.

With that purpose in mind, I trust that these mini-messages will help you as you serve God and His people. Since this material was published over a period of time, you will find some phrases and quotes repeated. Just accept this in the spirit of Philippians 3:1.

WARREN W. WIERSBE

1

In Praise of Plodders

Although he had only an elementary education, by the time he was in his teens, he could read the Bible in six languages. He later became Professor of Oriental Languages at Fort William College in Calcutta, and his press at Serampore provided Scriptures in over 40 languages and dialects for more than 300 million people.

His name? William Carey, "father of modern missions."

His secret? He was a plodder.

The one criterion

"Eustice," Carey said to his nephew, "if after my removal anyone should think it worth his while to write my life, I will give you a criterion by which you may judge of its correctness.

"If he gives me credit for being a plodder, he will describe me justly. Anything beyond this will be too much. I can plod. That is my only genius. I can persevere in any definite pursuit. To this I owe everything."

Getting your feet wet

The etymologists tell us that our word "plod" comes from an old Middle English word that means "a puddle." The Danish

11

have a similar word that means "mud." A "plodder" is someone who is willing to get his feet wet and wade through water and mud to get to his destination. He keeps going!

Shakespeare was wrong when he wrote, "Small have continual plodders ever won." History shows that it is the plodders who finally make it. "By perseverance," said Spurgeon, "the snail reached the ark."

In this age of fast food, digests and quick fixes, plodding is not held in high esteem; but it is still the plodders who are getting things done, a day at a time, a step at a time. Paul had the plodders in mind when he wrote: "And let us not lose heart in doing good, for in due time we shall reap if we do not grow weary" (Gal. 6:9).

Direction

Of course, the plodder needs to know where he is going, or his daily toil will be in vain. He doesn't want to become like the airline pilot who told the passengers, "We're lost, but we're making very good time!" It is important to have direction.

This means setting goals, definite goals, that may be measured. It also means breaking down those long-range goals into bite-size tasks that can be handled day by day. A Chinese proverb says, "The man who removed the mountain began by carrying away small stones." Don't be so dazzled by the distant destination that you get on the wrong path and lose your way.

Make a list of the things you feel God wants you to do, arrange them in order of priority, and use the list as a prayer guide and a road map for your ministry. It isn't necessary to share the whole list with everybody; some things are better kept quiet.

"When the pilot does not know what port he is heading for," says a Roman proverb, "no wind is the right wind." The pastor who has his destinations clearly in mind can adjust his sails as the winds change and still make it to the harbor.

Discipline

The plodder has to be disciplined. As he mended shoes, young William Carey taught himself Latin, Hebrew, Greek, French and Dutch. We might argue that he had a special gift for languages; but even if he did, his achievement at least encourages us to do more with the gifts God has given us. Persistence without ability is futility; but if God calls us to serve, He will equip us for the task.

Plodders have their eyes on the goal; they resist every effort to get them on a detour. "This one thing I do!" is their special verse (Phil. 3:13), and they will not change. David Sarnoff, president of RCA, said, "The will to persevere is often the difference between failure and success."

Divine encouragement

Isaiah 40:31 is a special promise for plodders. There are days when God enables us to soar like the eagle or run like the deer, but they are few and far between. However, when we wait each day on the Lord, He gives us the strength to plod: "They shall walk and not faint."

"God never communicates surplus power," said Joseph Parker. "God promises no strength beyond the day in which it is required." He cited Deuteronomy 33:25, the perfect text for the faithful plodder.

"Strength to walk may be yours," said Alexander Maclaren, "patient power for persistent pursuit of weary monotonous duty. That is the hardest, and so it is named last."

"Duty" is just another name for the will of God; and to Jesus, the will of God was satisfying food, not bitter medicine (John 4:34). When duty becomes delight, then plodding becomes pleasure; and the daily walk takes on new joy and excitement.

"Consider the postage stamp," said American wit Josh Billings. "Its usefulness consists in the ability to stick to one thing till it gets there."

Remember that the next time you open your mail.

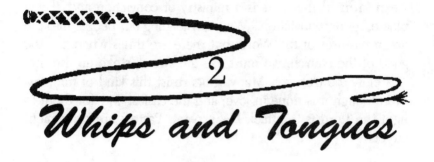

2
Whips and Tongues

"T he blow of a whip raises a welt, but a blow of the tongue crushes bones."

That statement from the Apocrypha (Ecclesiasticus 28:17) may not be inspired, but it is certainly true. How many times God's servants have been crushed by criticism, even to the point of wanting to resign from the church or to leave the ministry completely. They faithfully do their best and make sacrifices that only God can see, and what do they get in return? Cutting and crushing words of criticism that make them wonder, "Is it worth it all?"

Expect it

When it comes to criticism in the ministry, the first rule is: *Expect it.* After all, our Lord was unjustly criticized when He ministered, and there is no way His followers can escape the same treatment. He was lied about, slandered, blasphemed and openly ridiculed; and it all finally ended with a cross.

"The fellowship of His sufferings" is something the faithful minister must expect (Phil. 3:10). "Indeed, all who desire to live godly in Christ Jesus will be persecuted" (2 Tim. 3:12). It's a part

15

of the job description, so expect it. Satan will see to it that there will always be fires to put out.

The very nature of the ministry helps to invite criticism. Keep in mind that ours is a ministry of conviction and, if you please, "godly conviction." We enjoy leading our people into the green pastures of the Word; but there are times when, for the good of the church, we must use the sword, stoke up the fire, and blow the trumpet. Many saints resist this kind of ministry, even though it is done in love; and the easiest way for them to fight the Lord is to attack His servant. Pastors are convenient targets.

Evaluate it

"Consider the source" is often the first step in evaluating criticism. Not all church members really understand why they enjoy criticizing the pastor (or his wife and family). In too many instances, the causes are deep, and the problems have long and tangled roots. In spite of their faith, some believers are chronic critics for whom criticism is a way of life. Perhaps it helps them maintain their identity and position of importance in the fellowship. You pity them, but you still have to minister to them.

One of the best books on this subject is *Well-Intentioned Dragons* by Marshall Shelley, published by *Christianity Today* and Word Books. Another book that is older but still useful is *Neurotics in the Church* by Robert St. Clair (Revell).

Of course, not all criticism is bad, even if it is given to us in an unloving way by an unsympathetic person. "Never fear criticism," A.W. Tozer said. "If the critic is right, he has helped you. If he is wrong, you can help him. Either way, somebody gets helped."

This is a good piece of advice and one that can help us maintain a positive perspective in a negative and painful situation. But it is sometimes difficult to get the critic to accept this counsel and agree that he or she may be wrong! Even Paul had a hard time getting Euodias and Syntyche to face facts honestly (Phil. 4:2), and he had apostolic authority!

When Charles Spurgeon began his ministry in Waterbeach, he sometimes "shot from the hip" in his sermons without realizing the damage he was doing. A godly man wrote Titus 2:8 on a card ("sound in speech which is beyond reproach") and put it on the pulpit, and the young pastor got the message.

When he moved to London, Spurgeon had an unknown critic who sent him a weekly postcard listing the grammatical errors and other mistakes in each week's sermons. Spurgeon considered the service a kindness.

But grammatical errors and vicious criticism are two different things. A stab in the back is a far cry from a note on a postcard! We feel unjust criticism deeply, and we want to fight back. *But that may be just what the enemy wants us to do!* Years ago, a godly and experienced minister said to me, "Never kick a skunk. You may manufacture a worse problem than you started with." Wise advice indeed!

Wait on the Lord

Our immediate response to severe criticism may be to phone our friends in the church—or call another pastor—and gather our forces. But our first task is to quiet our own hearts and make sure we are ministering for the glory of the Lord and the good of the critic, and not for personal vengeance. A chat with a friend might help us calm down, but the peace we really need can come only from God.

(If you need some "medicine," try Isaiah 54:16,17, Psalms 34 and 37, Philippians 2:1-18 and Romans 12:9-21.)

This does not mean that we delay to act, because delay might give the enemy further opportunity to work. It only means that we are sure the Lord is in control of our lives as we seek to solve the problem. Ponder Proverbs 14:29 and 16:32, and learn to wait on God's timing.

Nothing defeats a critic faster than "speaking the truth in love" (Eph. 4:15). A calm confrontation in the fullness of the Spirit will do more to solve problems than any number of meetings where the old nature reigns.

And don't forget that Jesus said, "Make friends quickly with your opponent" (Matt. 5:25). This does not mean that we instantly capitulate and seek peace at any price. (Note James 3:13-18.) Rather, it means that we begin with some area of agreement and work from there. To start with our areas of conflict is to make matters worse.

The foe of flattery

It is a general rule that the person who is encouraged by praise will be devastated by criticism; so perhaps the place to start is with our own egos. Saintly Thomas 'a Kempis prayed, "Grant me prudently to avoid him that flatters me, and to endure patiently him that contradicts me." He learned that from Proverbs 27:6, a verse every minister ought to hide in his heart and heed in his life.

It does us good to face criticism from time to time, even though we may not enjoy it. Satan may want to use criticism as a weapon to batter us; but if we let Him, God can use it as a tool to build us. Sometimes God uses these difficult situations to purify His church and bring His true saints closer together. You may fight the battle and the next pastor claim the spoils; but either way, God's church is helped.

Vance Havner used to tell about the two men looking at a bird in the window of a taxidermist's shop. One man said, "That's sure a poor job of mounting a bird!" Just then the bird flew down from the perch!

Dr. Havner added, "The critics are often brought to shame when God upsets all their nice calculations!"

One pastor had a sign on his desk that read LOOK BEYOND THE CRITIC. It reminded him to see the Lord on the throne, to see the total church ministry and the many friends who loved him, and to see the purposes God wanted to achieve.

"To escape criticism," said Elbert Hubbard, "do nothing, say nothing, be nothing."

But is that the way Christ wants us to live?

3

Is It Really Worth It All?

A nyone who ministers for the Lord is bound to get weary and one day ask the question, "Is it really worth it all?" Preachers are human, too.

You take time away from your own family to help people, and they complain because you didn't come sooner and do more.

You go the extra ten miles to meet somebody's needs, and you never get one word of thanks.

You are on call twenty-four hours a day and often devote your day off to conducting a funeral, and people ask if you are busy.

You use a part of your vacation for study, and people wonder if you are working hard enough.

And there is always the specter of the former pastor ("What a great and godly man!") haunting every service and every board meeting.

Is it any wonder that you ask, "Is it really worth it all?"

Nothing new!

The question is not new, nor is the inward pain that goes with it. Moses gave his best to his people, and yet they criticized him as well as his wife. On one occasion, he told God he would rather die than lead the people of Israel, and he meant it.

Many of the saints of old, including the prophets and apostles, felt unappreciated and unwanted; and a roll call of the "great preachers" would reveal that they often felt the same way.

Apparently this is one of the occupational hazards of the ministry, so we had better expect it and learn to live with it. Phillips Brooks reminds us that growth in ministry means "higher heights of joy and deeper depths of sorrow," so our only escape is to stop growing.

Whom do we serve?

The place to start in dealing with this problem is in our own hearts. Before we can answer the question, "Is it worth it all?" we must ask, "Why am I ministering at all?" If we are ministering for any other reason than to serve the Lord, then nothing will make us happy.

The Jewish priests were set apart "to minister to the Lord" (Ex. 28:1, 3,4, 41). Of course, they served their people; but their first obligation was to please the Lord. Paul and Barnabas were ministering to the Lord when God called them into missionary service (Acts 13:2).

Yes, we serve God's people; but we serve them "for Jesus' sake" (2 Cor. 4:5). That means that our very first responsibility is to obey Him and please Him, *no matter what His people may say or do*. This should not make us independent in spirit, but rather dependent on the Lord and patient with His flock. After all, God is patient with us.

It is encouraging to know that the final judgment lies with our Master and not with His people. The Prophet Isaiah has

God's suffering servant say: "I have toiled in vain, I have spent My strength for nothing and vanity; yet surely the justice due to Me is with the Lord, and My reward with My God" (Isa. 49:4).

Paul took this same approach when dealing with the accusations of the militant crowd in Corinth (1 Cor. 4). It's the best approach to take.

Who's to blame?

It comes as a great relief when you realize that God's servants, if they are faithful in their ministry, are not held accountable for what their people do. If they were, then Moses and Paul are the two biggest failures in ministerial history!

God holds us accountable to do our work faithfully as He directs and as He enables, and the consequences are not in our hands. The pastor who expects all of his people to develop into spiritual giants is bound to be disappointed. For that matter, how many pastors become "giants"?

Don't forget faith

"Do you know what the formula is for blessing in ministry?" Dr. Lehman Strauss asked me many years ago. "It is to simply preach, and pray and *plug away!*" I've learned that he is right.

Ours is a ministry of faith, and we don't always see the results. The harvest is not the end of the meeting or of the church year. The harvest is the end of the age, and the Lord of the harvest will see to it that His good and faithful servants will get their just rewards.

The longer you minister, the better you understand that God has "seasons" to His work. He has a right time for everything, and everything is beautiful in its time (Eccles. 3:1-11). He uses different workers at different times to accomplish various purposes. A ministry you begin may be completed by somebody else, but both will share the reward and the joy of working together for Him (John 4:34-38).

The pastor who wants only to build a crowd, and not a church, doesn't have to work by faith. There are many surefire methods for entertaining the sheep and attracting the goats. But the minister who truly wants to edify the church must do his work by faith, and he will not always be able to measure the "results."

George Morrison said, "God rarely permits His servants to see all the good they are doing." When we wonder if it is really worth it all, we need to lay hold of His unchanging promise that "in due time we shall reap, if we do not grow weary" (Gal. 6:9).

Intimidation

The measurements for ministry are so confused these days that it's easy for any of us to be intimidated. (The fastest way to feel guilty is to attend a pastors' conference and listen to the speakers being introduced.) The discouragement that comes from intimidation (or envy) is one of Satan's chief weapons, and we must fight against it.

There are no small churches and there are no big preachers. All of us are important in the work of God, and He will see to it that no man's work will go unrecognized or unrewarded. Don't be too quick to praise another man's ministry, or to underrate your own. When tempted to do so, read and ponder 1 Corinthians 4:5.

As difficult as it is, we must try to separate feelings from facts. How we feel about the church and what God knows about the church, are two different things, as Revelation 2 and 3 make clear.

"Is it really worth it all?"

Yes, if you are doing it for the glory of the Lord. And the best part is, what you do will last forever.

4

The Minister Hurts

Somebody said something or did something and now the pastor hurts. From a human point of view, he has every right to hurt; but he knows that his people won't accept it. For some reason, pastors are supposed to "live above the snake line" and never have hurt feelings or broken hearts.

Quite the opposite is true. The loving "spiritual father and mother" (see 1 Thess. 2:7-12) who loves and cares for his family will be sensitive to what they say and do. All of us probably hurt our parents at one time or another when we were children, and the way they felt was an expression of their love. They were hurt.

When our people hurt, they come to us. Where do we go when we hurt?

As difficult as it is, we must make our own medicine and obey Matthew 5:10-12 and 43-48. Let's search our hearts to be sure that we have not sinned and given just cause for somebody

25

to criticize us. Preachers do make mistakes, and they also know how to make excuses for them. Excuses only make things worse. If an apology is in order, take care of the matter as soon as possible. Sometimes the best way to soar like an eagle is to learn to eat crow.

Patience and prayer

But suppose we discover that our hearts are clean in the matter? Then what? *Patience and prayer*. And while you are waiting and praying, evaluate the situation and ask God for wisdom.

Some things our people say and do are not worth noticing. If that's the case, the best thing you can do is to commit them to the Lord and forget about them. In his *Lectures to My Students*, Spurgeon urged pastors to have "a blind eye and a deaf ear," when it came to the common gossip and criticism in the church family. He said:

"You cannot stop people's tongues, and therefore the best thing is to stop your own ears and never mind what is spoken.

"Judge it to be a small matter what men think or say of you, and care only for their treatment of your Lord."

After all, perhaps the pastor himself occasionally says things he shouldn't say. Solomon may have had this in mind when he wrote, "Do not pay attention to every word people say, or you may hear your servant cursing you—for you know in your heart that many times you yourself have cursed others" (Eccl. 7:21-22 NIV). Sobering counsel!

"A man's discretion makes him slow to anger, and it is his glory to overlook a transgression" (Prov. 19:11).

Let the Lord do it...

But whether the pastor was right or wrong, he must forgive others and make sure his own heart is right with God and with God's people. If others won't wash the wounds they caused, let the Lord do it; otherwise those wounds will fester and cause pain and only create more trouble.

Positively the worst thing we can do is to perform a constant autopsy as we review the matter in our minds. This keeps the pain fresh and even adds to it, but it doesn't solve the problem. If anything, it makes it worse.

Fighting an ego problem within robs us of the peace and energy we need to love people and do our work well. Our families suffer, we suffer, and the church suffers. Is carrying a grudge worth all this suffering? The more we ponder the offense, the more we defend ourselves; and the more we defend ourselves, the more anxious we are to prove we are right. Then, when we least expect it, we launch our attack—and wish we had kept our mouths shut.

Explain but don't explode

This doesn't mean we shouldn't get it out of our system, but we must be careful to *explain* and not *explode*. Every pastor needs a friend with an open ear and a sympathetic heart who can listen and give encouragement. If we "talk it out," our hurt feelings will start to heal and our distorted vision will start to see things in perspective again.

President Harry Truman used to say to his colleagues, "If you can't take the heat, get out the kitchen!" We may not like it, but criticism is a part of the ministry; and the pastor with a thin skin or a sensitive ego has to learn how to take it.

To quote Spurgeon again: "You must be able to bear criticism, or you are not fit to be at the head of a congregation; and you must let the critic go without reckoning him among your deadly foes, or you will prove yourself a mere weakling."

Don't take yourself too seriously

This leads to another suggestion: *Don't take yourself too seriously*. A sense of humor is a powerful weapon to defeat the

Devil when he sets up a beachhead in your wounded heart. The ability to "laugh it off" has saved many leaders from the folly of trying to kill a mosquito with a cannon. You can do it, but plan to be picking up the pieces for weeks to come.

Yes, we take our office and our ministry seriously; but that's not the same as making ourselves so important that people can't disagree with us or criticize us. Often they don't even know that what they said or did cut us deeply; and when we tell them, they are usually more than willing to make things right.

It seems strange, but in many congregations there is often one member who just doesn't like the pastor. You go out of your way to love that person and try to win him or her over, but it just doesn't work. What should you do? Learn to cooperate with the inevitable and give your best to the whole church, without letting Saint Critic distract or disturb you. If you were an oyster, that abrasive bit of sand would help you manufacture a valuable pearl! You're not an oyster, but perhaps God can do the same for you!

5

The Pastor and Prayer

Many of us in ministry will confess that disciplined praying is one of our most difficult tasks. We know the importance of private prayer, and we are often called upon to pray in public; and yet the developing of a satisfying prayer life continues to be a challenge to us.

Put your mind at rest. The great saints of past ages had the same problem and probably never solved it. But there are some guidelines that all of us would do well to heed if we are to improve our prayer life.

What prayer is not

Prayer is not a spiritual technique for getting things done. It is the very circulatory system of ministry. "Without me, ye can do nothing" (John 15:5 KJV). Lack of prayer does not handicap us; it paralyzes us, whether we know it or not. The pastor of the church of Laodicea handed in excellent reports, but he did not realize that nothing lasting was really going on in his ministry.

The danger is not that we fail to pray, but that we may pray too much and not really mean it. The minister who prays during his morning devotional time, at meals, in homes and hospital rooms, and in public meetings, may easily become very professional in the whole matter. "Nothing is so deadening to the divine," wrote George Macdonald, "as an habitual dealing with the outside of holy things."

Personal prayer

If there is one place where personal prayer must not be "routine," it is in your own private devotional time. Like Jeremiah, the preacher can be bold before men only as he is broken and honest before God. (Read Jeremiah 8:18-9:3; 11:18-23; 12:1-6; 15:10-12, 15-21; 17:14-18; 18:18-23; 20:7-18.)

The Old Testament high priest bore the names of the tribes over his heart and on his shoulders, a picture of what the faithful pastor ought to be in his private ministry of prayer.

But let's not leave prayer in the closet; let's take it with us into the study. "To pray well is the better half of study," said Martin Luther. "I find commentaries very useful," said Spurgeon, "but, after all, many a text that will not open to a commentary will open to prayer." And Campbell Morgan said, "When all my attempts at exegesis fail, I worship."

Happy is that congregation whose pastor prays in the study, because he will bring quickening to a church. A message that is only "ground out" or (even worse) copied, will be merely a religious performance that will bring spiritual deadness.

I agree with Spurgeon that the minister ought to prepare his pastoral prayer. This does not mean that he writes it out and reads it to God and the people, but rather that he thinks it through and knows what he wants to say. There is sameness and tameness about most pulpit prayers. They are predictable, and perhaps ineffectual, although only the Lord knows.

A prepared preacher

When I was in the pastorate, I tried to reserve Saturday evenings to prepare myself for the spiritual duties of the Lord's Day. After all, what good is a prepared sermon if the preacher is not himself prepared? A part of this exercise was the outlining of the pastoral prayer so that from week to week there would be variety and vitality.

Many pastors follow a schedule for praying for missionaries so that none is forgotten over the course of the weeks. Of course, you always want to pray for those in authority, an admonition in Scripture that is often forgotten. One pastor we know centers each pastoral prayer on one attribute of God. The fact that we prepare does not limit the Spirit of God. After all, if we prepare the sermon, why not also prepare the pulpit prayer? Talking to God about His people is certainly as important as talking to His people about God.

Praying too often?

Some ministers pray too often in the Sunday services and they ought to invite others to share in this ministry. Surely others can pray for the offering or lead in intercession for special needs. However, the pastor must be careful to contact people in advance so that they may be prepared for this ministry.

If the minister is not careful, he will monopolize the praying in a worship service. He gives the invocation, leads in the pastoral prayer, prays for the offering, prays after the sermon, and then pronounces the benediction! Worship services should be carefully planned, and this includes those who participate in prayer.

The Pastor in Prayer is a collection of Spurgeon's pulpit prayers (Pilgrim Publications) and is worth reading—not to imitate but to gather inspiration. In the devotional section of your Christian bookstore, you should find volumes that contain the prayers of the "great saints," and these may encourage you in your own praying.

Whatever we do, we must be careful that our praying is not simply professional, but that it sincerely comes from our hearts. The prayer after the sermon should not review the message, and the benediction must not be a rehearsal of the announcements. Let prayer be prayer, and the Spirit of God will work in us and through us to accomplish His great purposes.

6

A Pastor's Prayer

This prayer by Thomas à Kempis is worth meditating on—and using—in the pastor's own devotional time:

"Thou, O God, who givest Grace to the Humble, do something also for the Proud Man: Make me Humble and Obedient; take from me the Spirit of Pride and Haughtiness, Ambition and Self-Flattery, Confidence and Gayety; Teach me to think well, and to expound all things fairly of my Brother, to love his worthiness, to delight in his Praises, to excuse his Errors, to give Thee thanks for his Graces, to rejoice in all the good that he receives, and ever to believe and speak better things of him than of myself.

"O Teach me to love, to be concealed and little esteemed, let me be truly humbled and heartily ashamed of my Sin and Folly. Teach me to bear Reproaches evenly, for I have deserved them; to return all to Thee, for it is Thine alone; to suffer Reproach thankfully; to amend my faults speedily, and when I have humbly, patiently, charitably, and diligently served Thee, change this Habit into the shining Garment of Immortality, my confusion into Glory, my Folly into perfect Knowledge, my Weakness and Dishonors into the Strength and Beauties of the Sons of God. Amen."

7

The Minister Alone

T he most important part of our lives is the part that only God sees, that "inner life" of the soul that nourishes the "outer life" everyone can see. Call it what you will—the devotional life, the "morning watch," the quiet time—the pastor's private life with God is the secret of Christian character, the source of power for service, the lifeline of all that the pastor must be and do.

That heroic missionary, Henry Martyn, wrote in his journal: "Let me be taught that the first great business on earth is the sanctification of my own soul; so shall I be rendered more capable of performing the duties of the ministry in a holy solemn manner."

Like the Jewish priest of old, we first of all serve God (Ex. 28:1,4, 41). Yes, we have a ministry to God's people, but our first responsibility is to be holy before the Lord and seek to please Him. Only then can we adequately serve His people.

The pastor faces problems in this area that his parishioners may not face. For one thing, he is involved in "holy things" all day long. He studies the Bible. He visits people and prays with them, sometimes interceding five or six times a day as he makes his pastoral rounds. He reads theological books and magazines.

While he is not isolated from the realities of life, his constant exposure to spiritual things can create problems.

The problem of professionalism

The greatest problem, of course, is professionalism. George MacDonald wrote: "Nothing is so deadening to the divine as an habitual dealing with the outside of holy things." We must be sure that our praying in the hospital room is sincere, not routine, and that our reading of the Word in a home is meaningful to us.

A vibrant devotional life can deliver the busy minister from the kind of perfunctory service that spreads death instead of life. As he meets with the Lord at the beginning of each day, he discovers new delight in the Word and in fellowship with the Lord. This is a time that must be guarded jealously!

The problem of intimidation

Another problem is intimidation. We read about the "great saints" of old and despair because our prayer life does not measure up to theirs. Spurgeon admitted that he had only twice spent a whole night in prayer; and Moody said that he tried to pray all night, and when he woke up, his bones ached!

You must develop the style of devotional life that best satisfies your needs. The important thing is discipline. Work out your approach and stick with it. It has well been said, "Beware of the barrenness of a busy life." Unless we start the day with the Lord, other things will intrude and the fresh manna will have melted by the time we get around to picking it up.

The problem of flexibility

As your family life changes, your devotional time may have to be adjusted. Be flexible, but be determined. Your daily meeting with the Lord is not a luxury; it is a necessity.

Each day's experience will be different because each day's

needs and demands are different, and the Lord knows how to prepare us. We should have a systematic schedule for reading the Word and meditating on it. Some ministers like to use a hymnal along with their Bible. A good devotional book, one that gives you something more solid than a verse, a "thought" and a prayer, can also be a help; but it must never become a substitute for your Bible.

My Utmost for His Highest by Oswald Chambers is excellent for the Christian worker, and so are the books by Amy Carmichael. Andrew Murray is a favorite of many. Keep in mind that the devotional book only "primes the pump"; it is not the major source of Living Water.

Beware the "religious routine"!

We must beware of a "religious routine" that is only a pseudo-devotional life: We read the Scriptures, we read a devotional meditation, we go through our prayer list, and we go away no better than we came. No, we go away *worse* than we came because we have fooled ourselves into thinking we have had a spiritual experience with the Lord.

Perhaps this is one reason why God allows His servants to suffer and to have "church problems." Nothing causes a minister to turn to the Word and take time to pray like a personal experience of challenge or suffering. Martin Luther said that prayer, meditation and suffering make a minister; and certainly he would know!

Some pastors find it meaningful to change translations as they read the Word. We get very familiar with the translation we preach from regularly, and this could rob us of blessing as we seek to feed our own souls. Each man must make his own decision here, and no one can dictate for another.

Dr. John R.W. Stott wrote in *Between Two Worlds*, a book every preacher should read once a year: "Nothing will more quickly rid us of laziness and coldness, of hypocrisy, cowardice and pride than the knowledge that God sees, hears and takes account" (p. 339).

And He waits to meet us—alone—each day.

8

Minister in a Corner

Every minister needs a corner, a quiet place where he can retreat from the duties of the day, where he can be himself and find himself, as he communes with God

Not a place for him to study theology or to prepare sermons. Rather, a place where he can be still enough to hear God speak within, a place where he can get better acquainted with God and with himself, a place where joyful worship can well up within him as he enjoys God.

A manufactured ministry?

All of us are too busy. Our bodies run ahead of our souls, and we start to rip apart at the seams. We become so involved in helping others that we neglect the Source of our help—and then we ourselves need help. Slowly, we start to manufacture ministry instead of bear fruit, because the life within us has been neglected.

It's not enough for us to depend solely on our morning quiet time, as important as that is in the life of every believer, and especially the pastor. We need to "take time to be holy" in the midst of the busy day. After all, we take coffee breaks; so why not take "blessing breaks"?

A quiet corner?

I have a "quiet corner" in our home where I retreat only for prayer, devotional reading, worship and the spiritual nourishment of my own soul. I do no studying there; I prepare no sermon outlines (although I do write down whatever ideas may come); I make no plans; I solve no problems. All I do is invest a few minutes—the length of time varies—centering my thoughts on God and making sure my heart is happy in Him.

This is not my main devotional time. It is an interlude, a "blessing break," a parenthesis that steadies and strengthens me for the work yet to be done. I try to go there at least once each day.

Of course, your "quiet corner" need not be in your home. ("A quiet corner in *our* house?" I hear some pastor ask.) Perhaps the best place for you is at the church, or the public library, or in the front seat of your car. So be it; but just be sure it is the best place for you. The important thing is that the place be devoted *only* to the spiritual discipline of communing with your Lord. If you do anything else there, you may rob yourself of enrichment.

Have available the resources that help you the most: a Bible, a hymnal, one or two classic books of Christian devotion. I keep in my "quiet corner" *The Imitation of Christ*, Fenelon's *Spiritual Letters*, Joe Bayly's *Psalms of My Life*, and (from time to time, as I sense the need) a book of short devotional messages. George Morrison is a favorite; so is George Matheson.

A time to focus

The important thing is that I calm my soul before God and focus on Him alone—not on my work, my problems or my needs. I begin with praise, using one of the Psalms and emphasizing the character of God. I lift my heart and seek to express joyful worship in the Spirit.

The great danger is that we use our "blessing break" as an escape from life, when in reality it is a preparation for life. "God is our refuge *and strength*" (Psalm 46:1, italics mine). We take refuge in Him, not to be sheltered from life, but to be strengthened for life with its many demands and duties. To be "under His wings" does not mean to be out of His work or avoiding His will!

"Blessing" breaks

The minister who tells himself that he is "too busy" to invest time in this way is actually confessing that his priorities are confused. His first obligation in life is to worship God and cultivate the sanctity of his own soul. And it is amazing how much easier the "wheels of mortal life" turn when we take time to be holy.

Get into the habit of saying to yourself each day, "It's time to take a blessing break!" Retreat to your quiet corner, commune with the Lord, meditate on His Word, worship Him, and let Him renew your strength.

9

Room to Grow In

"T he trouble with you preachers," said the doctor, "is that you really don't practice what you preach. You tell other people to obey the laws of God and you don't obey them yourself.

"My suggestion is that you stop burning the candle at both ends and start taking time off for rest and relaxation. You'll live longer and do a better job."

We were ministering in Chicago when my doctor preached that sermon to me, and he was right. The schedule I was trapped in was both tempting God and destroying me. But when you are a workaholic, what do you do?

Understand what relaxation is

The English word "leisure" comes from a Latin word that means "to be permitted." Leisure time is time that we control, time that we have set aside for ourselves, come what may. We don't feel guilty for enjoying it, because we know we need it and God wants us to have it.

It is definitely not *wasted time*, when you wear yourself out worrying about doing nothing. Nor is it only *free time* that you have earned because you have worked so hard and been a good Christian.

Each week, most of our people have the Lord's Day—plus a day off—for relaxation and re-creation; but the busy pastor works harder on Sunday than on any other day. And as for that day off, well, one crisis in the church family can quickly claim it.

"I have no sympathy with those who say the Devil never takes a vacation," said the late Vance Havner. "I am not following the Devil but the Lord who said, 'Come ye yourselves apart and rest a while.' If you don't come apart, you will come apart—and you'll go to pieces."

Understand why you need it

Obviously, your body needs a time of rest and re-creation; otherwise it starts to rebel and create problems for you and the people with whom you live and work. No matter what kind of insurance you have, good health is much cheaper than good coverage.

How strange it is that servants of God, who would never think of using tobacco, alcohol or narcotics, will nevertheless follow a schedule that produces stress, physical damage and eventual burnout.

Your mind needs relaxation. The most gifted person can't do creative work under constant pressure. The work of the ministry is tough; and if the Lord is going to give us what we need as preachers and pastors, we must take time to wait and listen. We need margins in our lives, occasions when time stands still and eternity takes over. We need room to grow in.

Doctors tell us that burnout is "the product of unresolved emotional conflict." It's not the demands of our work that destroy us, but the way we respond to those demands. Many a pastor has listened to his nerves instead of to the Lord and ended up looking for a new vocation, when what he really needed was a vacation. If you value your emotional life, take time to relax. Don't become a martyr by blowing all your fuses at once.

"Be still, and know that I am God" (Psalm 46:10 KJV) is a command. If you want to know God, you have to take time to wait before Him. It's amazing how the Lord brings spiritual refreshing when we take time for creative relaxation, to think, to meditate and pray, to read, to laugh, to enjoy . . . and not feel guilty about it.

Understand what hinders it

Let's start with *pride*. We are so important that we can't take a day off, or even a few hours off, after an afternoon of intensive visiting or counseling. The church might fall apart during our nap. There are pastors who phone Dial-A-Prayer daily to see if there are  any messages for them, but they eventually learn that they are not God. Sometimes they learn it in the cardiac ward of the hospital where the tuition is very high.

Another hindrance to creative leisure is *fear*. The insecure pastor must show his people that he is very busy; otherwise, they may fire him. The fear of man still brings a snare (see Prov. 29:25), and the first evidence that we are trapped is our desire to please everybody. The perfect epitaph for this minister is, "He was beloved by everybody, but he did not know how to say NO."

"He did not learn to delegate" might be another suitable epitaph for the minister who didn't have time to rest but who did find time to die. After all, other people in the church have spiritual gifts and should be given opportunities to exercise them. Let your people grow as they help you carry the load. You'll be better off.

Sometimes it's a *false view of ministry* that robs you of leisure time. "I must win the whole world!" is both a noble ideal and a shortcut to the hospital. "I'd rather burn out than rust out!" sounds spiritual, but are those the only alternatives? Why not just "work out" your own salvation as God works in you (see Phil. 2:12-13) and keep going as long as you can?

Some principles to follow

Let's start with the ancient adage "Know thyself." What is your best time for study? When do your "creative juices" really flow? Never mind how Spurgeon or Billy Sunday did it. What schedule is best for you? Once you have determined this, share it with the church leaders *and tell them why*. If you feed the flock from the green pastures of the Word, they will be glad you are taking time to relax and experience re-creation.

Plan your work and practice saying "No" in a gracious way. The younger pastor may have a problem here, but it's not impossible. We serve the Lord as His servants, and a part of our obedience to Him is that we take care of our body, His temple.

Get a head start on the day by getting up earlier and having a satisfying devotional time. When we rush into the day, we often create our own problems. Live a day at a time and take some time each day to be alone for relaxation and renewal. Even thirty minutes invested this way can do wonders for your outlook and your outcome!

We recommend Gordon MacDonald's *Ordering Your Private World* (Nelson), which has now been reissued in an expanded edition. Read it and take its message to heart. After all, if you and the Lord don't control your time, then somebody else will; and the results may be disastrous. Your home, your life and your ministry can take on a whole new atmosphere of enrichment and enjoyment if only you will learn to balance work with relaxation.

10

The Discouraged Minister

We don't have space enough in this chapter to go into all the details of ministerial burnout, its causes and cures; but it might help to drop a few hints that may help some faithful servant who is about to throw in the towel.

1. *Take care of your body.* Late hours, overweight, fast-food lunches, constant pressure—all these can create physical problems that affect your mind and emotions. Sometimes the most spiritual thing you can do is take a nap! (Consider Elijah in 1 Kings 19.) Your body is God's temple and God's tool—take care of it. You need a day off and a vacation, just like any other workman.

2. *Plan your work.* Nothing weighs us down like unfinished work, especially tasks we don't enjoy doing. If you don't plan your work (and work your plan), those evangelical emergencies that always come will leave you without time enough to get your regular work finished. Plan your preaching and try to do your studying (not the final outline) two weeks in advance.

3. *Discipline your time.* We who deal with eternity can be great wasters of time. Get to your study an hour early one day a week, before the phone starts ringing, and you will get a day's work done. Beware of long lunches and extended coffee breaks. Make a list of things to do each day, and do them.

4. *Minister by faith.* George Morrison used to say, "God rarely allows His servants to see all the good they are doing." The harvest is the end of the age, not the end of the meeting. Sow the seed and trust God for the increase in His time. Galatians 6:9 is still in the inspired Word.

5. *Talk to somebody you trust.* It was when Elijah was alone that he started to fall apart. Don't keep it all bottled up; let somebody bear the burdens with you. Get a prayer partner and meet once a week.

6. *Look beyond the critic.* You can't please everybody, nor should you try. Don't take every failure personally; next month, the Board may *accept* the idea that they rejected this month. Don't lose your perspective over one little matter.

7. *Maintain your spiritual life.* We who are "in the Word" constantly must take time to nurture our own souls. Read the Bible, not to find sermons but to find sustenance for your own life. Occasionally read a sermon from a master preacher, not to get ideas but to hear from God.

8. *Avoid self-pity!* Once it begins, it spreads like a forest fire. Don't take yourself too seriously; learn how to laugh at yourself. Elijah thought he was the only faithful one left—but he was wrong.

9. *Live for others.* You double your joy when you share another's burden.

11

To Go or Not to Go?

I f the servant of God is at all faithful, he is frequently
examining both himself and his ministry and honestly asking
the question, "Is it time for me to make a move?" The
issue is not career advancement, more money or the desire
to escape from difficult problems. (There are difficult
problems in *every* church; only the names and faces
change.) No, the real issue is the will of God—what is best
for God's people and God's servant.

Except in those unfortunate churches where the ministry
is only a job, the relationship between pastor and people is a
close one that cannot be ruptured without pain. Therefore, it
behooves both pastor and people to face this matter humbly and
in the fear of God. For the pastor and his family, working through
the question, "Shall I go or stay?" can be either an agonizing
experience of paralyzing pain or an edifying experience of growth.
To be sure, any decision of this nature is always painful, but the
pain need not be permanent or damaging.

Here are some suggestions the perplexed pastor may want
to consider as he goes through the throes of evaluation that may
lead to resignation.

49

Know yourself

Some men are equipped for longer ministries, and some are not. It is my guess that too many pastors leave too soon and that both they and their churches might have been stronger if they had stayed longer. Some pastors are pioneers who can clear the brush and plant the seed, but they have a tough time tending the garden. We are all different: some plow, some sow, some water, and some harvest; but it is God who gives the increase.

What are your special gifts? Are they what the church needs at this time in its history? Have you and the people "grown comfortable together" so that the challenge is gone? Or are you only discouraged and perhaps seeking an excuse to run away? Is there some problem that you don't want to face and solve or some new vision for the ministry that frightens you? Be honest!

Only you can answer these questions. This does not mean that you cannot consult with others whose spiritual insight you respect, because honest confrontation with other hearts and minds (and be sure to include your wife!) can help you better understand yourself. However, the "buck" stops with you, so don't try to avoid it.

Know the signs

The pastor does not "change jobs" the way most other workers do. God builds both the worker and the work. They are intimately tied together, and what happens to the shepherd is certain to affect the sheep.

As you look over your field and your work, ask yourself:

1) Are the challenge and excitement gone in my heart?
2) Am I reacting or responding?
3) Am I planning ahead or just treading water?
4) Do I enjoy being away from my own pulpit?
5) Are some of my best leaders—not the "cranks"— starting to hint about change?

6) Am I personally growing in my own spiritual life and professional skills, or do I resist change?
7) How am I responding to honest criticism?
8) Am I watching the clock and the calendar and no longer making personal sacrifices for the good of the work?

Depending on what you see and how you feel, you may give different answers at different times; but when some definite conclusions start to take shape, you will be that much closer to a decision.

Know the field

It is never easy for us to know when our own work is done. Just about the time we think we have failed, God gives evidence that He is blessing. However, we must be honest with ourselves and the Lord and seek to evaluate our ministry.

How would a change in pastors affect programs that are now going on? Are there special problems that your experience equips you to handle best? Or is there a desperate need for a new perspective and a breath of fresh air?

Is the situation such that your successor could fit in easily? Is the church at such a level spiritually and organizationally that change would not be a threat, even though it might bring a certain amount of pain? And what about the people you are counseling or disciplining?

In your sanctified imagination, project yourself and the church down the road about five years. What do you see for them and for you? Does what you see excite you? Can you see yourself as part of it?

No pastor can do everything, but have you finished the work that God gave *you* to do? And are things ready for a new man to take the work even further? Would the next man have an easier time if you waited six months or a year? It is best for everyone involved if the pastor "quits while he is ahead." Better to sail out on the crest of a wave than to linger too long and be drowned. Be sure that your wife and family are in agreement as you have prayed and talked together. A move will be serious for your children, so don't minimize their feelings. The important thing is that you are going to a new ministry and not simply *leaving* a ministry.

Know how to cooperate

Work in harmony with your church leaders. Resignations don't create problems—they *reveal* them. Set a schedule that is agreeable to you and the church family, and stick to it. Be decisive, and turn a deaf ear to the dear people who ask you to reconsider. They said the same thing to the last pastor and will probably say it to the next one when he leaves.

Finally, get out of the way of your successor and try to be an encouragement to him. Don't go back to the field for weddings, funerals or other reasons without contacting him. Treat him the way you want your predecessor to treat you when you arrive at your new field.

Changes are never easy, and they get harder as we grow older. Handle your situation so that, with God's help, you will be able to look back with joy and look ahead with excitement.

12

Formula for Frustration

M inisters are human beings, made of dust, subject to the same forces that discourage and destroy men and women who sit in the pews. For some reason, many church members have the idea that their pastor is exempt from personal pressures and problems—or that he has a secret system for overcoming the difficulties of life and ministry. He does not.

The tragedy is not that pastors collapse, burn out or even fail. The tragedy is that too many sincere Christian workers bring these things on themselves. How? By failing to detect, identify and deal with the elements that make up the "formula for frustration." Here they are:

Unreachable goals

Now that secular management principles have invaded the church, everybody is talking about goals. Fine; we need goals. As the Latin proverb says, "When the pilot does not know what port he is heading for, no wind is the right wind." Substitute the word "pastor" and the message is clear.

But goals must be sensible and reachable; otherwise, we only tempt God. If you determined this year's goals after listening to a super-pastor at a conference, give serious thought to revising them. If you measure your ministry on the basis of unreachable goals, you are bound to give up or become impossible to live with—or both!

Unmanageable schedules

You can't attend every meeting, make every visit, speak at every special occasion, read every book, hold every office or solve every problem. Find out what God wants you to do, assign the rest to others—and learn how to say "No!" It will shock folks at first, but before long they will get the idea, and they will appreciate the fact that you have priorities.

Make a list of the things you as pastor must do, and schedule regular time for these tasks: your personal devotional life, family time, study, sermon preparation, administration and so on. Try to do your vital sermonic "spadework" two weeks in advance, just in case there is an emergency. (There usually is.) When you find yourself fighting time, you know you have put too much on the calendar and you cannot do your best.

Uncomfortable situations

We all have them! The best approach is to take to heart the words of the famous prayer: "God grant me the serenity to accept things I cannot change, courage to change the things I can and wisdom to know the difference." Amen and amen!

Sometimes it's good to have a blind eye and a deaf ear and not take too seriously what some people in the church say and do. This does not mean we are careless in our pastoral work; it only means we don't try to use a cannon to kill a flea. If you take too personally what people say, you will become a nervous wreck. Many of these people will not change—and they will act the same way toward the next pastor! It isn't your fault. Stop feeling guilty.

In time, some people and situations will start to change. Never give up! A friend used to say to me, "Just preach and pray and plug away!" Excellent counsel—and it works!

Unbearable problems

The younger minister sometimes has a "messianic complex." He has to solve every problem and do it immediately. Then he learns that solving some problems is like unscrambling eggs or loading mercury with a pitchfork. Yes, God often graciously does the impossible, and we simply stand by in awe. But when that doesn't happen, what does the pastor do?

He walks and works by faith and leaves the consequences with God. He does not measure his ministry by the number of success cases in his files. He accepts the sad fact that some folks don't want their problems solved; they need their problems to give them a feeling of importance. Jesus could not do many miracles in Nazareth, His hometown, because the people would not believe. Where does that leave us?

George Morrison has said that God rarely allows His servants to see how much good they are doing, so you will have to work by faith and leave the results with Him. We'll get the report and the reward when we stand before Him in Glory, not one minute before. Meanwhile, let's not permit these four "frustration factors" to add to our burdens and rob us of joy and power in our ministry.

You may quote...

- Never let good books take the place of the Bible. Drink from the Well, not from the streams that flow from the Well. —*Amy Carmichael*

- Great Services reveal our possibilities; little services reveal our consecration. —*George H. Morrison*

- He overcomes the frustration of the times whose plans and purposes belong to God. —*Anonymous*

- A good definition of frustration: Missing your turn in a revolving door. —*Anonymous*

- All God's giants have been weak men who did great things for God, because they reckoned on God being with them. —*J. Hudson Taylor*

- God's best gifts are not in things but in opportunities. —*Anonymous*

- Many men owe the grandeur of their lives to their tremendous difficulties. —*Charles Haddon Spurgeon*

- Intellect gives form to feeling, feeling gives warmth to conscience, and conscience gives basis to both. —*John Ker*

- No man shall ever behold the glory of Christ by sight hereafter who doth not in some measure behold it by faith here in this world. Grace is a necessary preparation for glory, and faith for sight. —*John Owen*

13

For Those
Who Hurt

"Why don't you think about doing a series on suffering?" an elder asked me. "Many of our people are hurting, and the Bible has a lot to say about God's help for hurting people."

The idea "took" and I preached seven messages on the subject. In fact, much of the material ended up in my book *Why Us? When Bad Things Happen to God's People* (Revell). The response to the sermons (which I have used often in conferences) and to the book would encourage me to urge you to consider such a series.

Dangers

However, before you announce the series in the next church bulletin, stop long enough to consider some hard facts.

First, this is not easy preaching; so give yourself time to read, think, pray and organize. A surface view of suffering in the Bible is not what people need, and that is often what is easiest to give them. We dare not become "Job's comforters" with easy answers to difficult questions.

This leads to a *second* warning: Don't major on explanations or your series will be very brief. After all, we do not live on explanations; we live on promises. As I prepared to write *Why Us?*, I read scores of books on suffering, by philosophers and theologians, by sufferers of one kind or another, by religious leaders of many persuasions, saved and unsaved; and they all came to just about the same conclusion: We can't explain everything and we have to live by faith. Faith in what? Well, not all of them answered that one!

Third, avoid bringing the academic into the pulpit, and this includes the learned arguments about the origin of evil and why a loving God permits suffering in His world. Suffering is a fact of life, and all our "explaining" will not make our listeners feel any better or face life with greater courage. Please don't turn the church into a lecture hall for the brainy. Let it be a holy sanctuary where hurting people can get a fresh view of God and a new supply of His grace.

Finally, be sure you and God are getting along when it comes to this matter of suffering. Have you ever really suffered yourself? Do you know personally something of what other people are going through? Is your own heart broken because of the sorrow and seeming tragedy in today's world? Do you nurture any hidden grudges against God because of hurts that have not healed? Honest preaching on suffering is a kind of "spiritual therapy" for the preacher who wants to be at his best for God.

Your people will not be fooled for long, so get ready! Nothing reveals the preacher's heart like a sermon on suffering. How easy it is to say the right things in the right way but leave something lacking. Heart? Sympathy and understanding? The kind of tenderness you get only in the furnace? Love? A willingness to leave some questions unanswered?

Finally—and you already know this—keep the personal experiences of your people out of the pulpit. As the dying lady said to her pastor, "Please don't make a story out of me!" There is nothing wrong with inviting your people to share their testimonies of how God helped them in the valley—or even with including some of your own experiences. Just be sure not to betray confidences, and see that God gets the glory. Try to focus on God and what He can do for people like us.

Approaches

The creative minister can take one of several approaches in dealing with such a vast subject as suffering.

1. *Sufferers in the Bible.* Job, Abraham, Jacob, Rachel, Moses, David, Jeremiah, Hosea, Paul, Mary and a host of Bible greats help us better understand what God can do for us when we are hurting. Each one suffered for a different reason and in a different way. Don't try to cover all that happened in their lives; just focus on the main ideas.

2. *God's promises for sufferers.* You probably have your favorite verses, and you might even be able to gather favorite promises from your people. You could even include in the service the testimony of the person who suggested that promise for that message. Don't ignore the familiar tried-and-true promises or search for obscure texts. Stick to the clear road markers that God's saints have followed for centuries.

3. *Questions about suffering.* This is a safe approach as long as you don't give the impression that you know all the answers to all the hard questions about suffering. Again, we live by promises and not by explanations. But the Christian faith is reasonable, and we need not dodge tough questions, even if we cannot explain everything.

Why do the righteous suffer and the wicked seem to escape? (Try Psalm 73 for this one.) Are suffering and love incompatible? How do believers pray about suffering? (Try 2 Corinthians 12:1-10.) What is Jesus doing now for those who suffer? How does the Lord "heal the brokenhearted"? How can we help people bear their sorrows? How does knowing you are going to heaven help you bear life's burdens today?

These are not easy questions, and you dare not pass out pat answers that only say to people, "The pastor doesn't really understand." This is one series that must *grow* within you; it must not be manufactured.

Resources

Your best sources are your Bible, your own heart and what you learn in the valley with your people, including your family. Yes, sometimes the Lord puts the preacher himself in the furnace to help him make his sermons warm and glowing! Give yourself time, and the series will mature; and you will know just when it is "ripe."

In listing these books, I am not endorsing everything in them. My only recommendation is that I found them helpful. If one of your favorite books is missing from this list, it does not mean I have banned it. Some of the books have bibliographies.

Baker, Don: *Depression* and *Pain's Hidden Purpose* (Multnomah).

Billheimer, Paul E.: *Don't Waste Your Sorrows* (Christian Literature Crusade).

Claypool, John: *Tracks of a Fellow Struggler* (Word).

Epp, Theodore: *Why Do Christians Suffer?* (Back to the Bible).

Gerstenberger, E.S., and Schrage, W.: *Suffering*, in the "Biblical Encounter Series" (Abingdon).

Hopkins, Hugh E.: *The Mystery of Suffering* (Inter-Varsity Press).

Lewis, C.S.: *The Problem of Pain* (Geoffrey Bles).

Meyer, F.B.: *The Gift of Suffering* (Kregel).

Peterson, Michael: *Evil and the Christian God* (Baker).

Plantinga, Theodore: *Learning to Live With Evil* (Eerdmans).

Smith, A.E. Wilder: *The Paradox of Pain* (Harold Shaw).

Strauss, Lehman: *In God's Waiting Room* (Moody Press).

Wenham, John W.: *The Enigma of Evil* (Zondervan).

Wiersbe, Warren (compiler): *Classic Sermons on Suffering* (Kregel).

Yancey, Philip: *Where Is God When It Hurts?* (Zondervan).

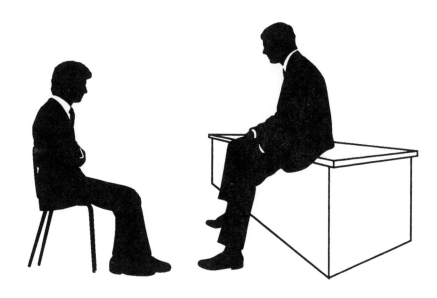

14

The Pastor As Listener

We commonly think of the pastor as a *speaker*, but he also needs to be a listener. In fact, the pastor who doesn't know how to *listen* creatively is not going to do as good a job *speaking* creatively.

I'm thinking of a younger pastor who often sought my counsel, but was rarely benefited by it. The reason? He did not take time to listen. No sooner would I begin to make an observation or answer a question, than he would launch into his next problem. I often wondered what his approach was in counseling situations.

Most of us in ministry are so sure of our answers that we have a difficult time hearing people out. We think of a verse to quote or a bit of personal experience to share. In fact, we are so busy with our own thoughts that we really don't give our full attention to the speaker. As a result, we end up giving superficial advice instead of helpful spiritual counsel.

We need to heed Solomon's words: "He who gives an

answer before he hears, it is folly and shame to him" (Prov. 18:13).

Pride

Perhaps a part of our problem is pride. After all, *we* are the experts! *We* know the Word of God! No need for anyone to go into detail; for, after all, we have had a great deal of experience and we can categorize and analyze almost any problem immediately!

Except that the problem the person starts with isn't always the problem that is really on his or her heart. It is the loving listener who gains the confidence of the person and who eventually gets to the roots of the real problem.

Patience

Yes, listening takes patience and humility, and a great deal of love; and one of the best ways to cultivate these three spiritual qualities is to practice good listening. We must pray that God will enable us to be "swift to hear, slow to speak, slow to wrath" (James 1:19).

It is especially important that we be good listeners in the casual contacts of life. In pastoral ministry, no contact is unimportant or routine. A good listener can detect, even in "passing conversation," feelings that ought to be dealt with. When I was in pastoral ministry, I always arrived at services early (especially the evening service) and walked throughout the auditorium, chatting with people. I do this still in conference ministry. Why? For one thing, it gives me that personal contact with the people that I need when I get into the pulpit. But it also helps me find out where the people are and what is on their hearts.

Part of the program

We must also be good listeners in the "official" contacts of ministry, including those sometimes exasperating board and committee meetings. The wise "listening pastor" can learn a great deal about his people, especially the church leaders, if he practices James 1:19 in official meetings.

Sometimes we are so anxious to get our "program" across that we don't take time to listen to what others have to say. The new pastor in particular needs to listen to the people who have read the minutes of the previous meeting and know some of the pitfalls that lie ahead. Even if we disagree with their thinking, the fact that we have listened to them makes it easier for them to listen to us.

Counselors discover that the more they listen—*really* listen—the more people will talk to them. When troubled people discover that you are concerned enough to hear them out, they will talk. And when they find that you are not interrupting with scoldings, free advice and useless observations, they feel more confident with you.

Yes, for those of us who are called to speak, it is difficult to listen; but we must cultivate both a listening ear and a listening heart. Zeno of Citium, who lived 300 years before Christ, said, "The reason why we have two ears and only one mouth is that we may listen the more and talk the less."

He had the right idea.

15

Wake Up and Preach!

"The sin of being uninteresting," writes Bishop William Quayle, "is in a preacher an exceedingly mortal sin. It hath no forgiveness." (*The Pastor-Preacher*: Baker, p. 140.)

When we consider the excitement of the drama of redemption, we wonder that *any* sermon would ever be boring, but alas, many of them are.

Excitement wanted

Dorothy Sayers wrote, "The Christian faith is the most exciting drama." The preacher who makes Bible doctrine dull understands neither the doctrine he is preaching nor the people he is preaching to.

It is difficult to preach anything that does not really excite you. The psalmist bubbled over with what he had to say (Psalm 45:1), and Jeremiah spoke as a man who had fire in his bones (Jer. 20:9). Unless the preacher is alive with his message, the congregation will not get excited.

This does not mean that the man in the pulpit substitutes energy for unction and sensationalism for truth. Abraham Lincoln said he liked to hear a man preach as though he were swatting bees! But Lincoln knew, as we all do, that mere activity can never take the place of true ministry. All Lincoln said was, "I want to hear a man preach who is really *alive* in the pulpit."

Fire in the pulpit

Woe to the congregation whose minister preaches only because it is Sunday and he has to say something! Blessed is that assembly whose pastor can hardly wait to deliver what God has said to his soul. Of course, the fire is lit in the place of prayer and in the study, and then it is taken to the pulpit.

When the pastor is bored with the Bible and the Christian life and is weary of his ministry or his people, this attitude will show up in his messages. It is one thing to become tired *in* the Lord's work and quite something else to become tired *of* the Lord's work. "And let us not be weary in well doing."

Just as the Old Testament priest went to the altar early each morning, removed the cold ashes, lit a fresh fire, and laid the burnt offering on it, so the minister must daily keep the fire burning on the altar of his heart. Paul urged Timothy to "stir up" the gift of God that was in him (2 Tim. 1:6), and the words mean to rekindle a flame and get it blazing.

Why do fires go out?

The usual cause of a dying fire is neglect. That explains why Paul wrote Timothy, "Do not neglect the spiritual gift within you" (1 Tim. 4:14). If the priest neglected the altar and forgot the daily burnt offering, the fire would go out.

"Let me be taught that the first great business on earth is the sanctification of my own soul." Henry Martyn wrote that in his journal, and he was right. Not sanctification for our own sake, of course, but for the sake of Jesus Christ and the people to whom we minister (John 17:17-21).

Growth wanted

The growing minister, facing new challenges in both his life and his church, will usually be excited about what God is saying to him and doing for him. At an athletic event, you can be a spectator and still get excited; but it doesn't work that way in the ministry. You have to be in the arena yourself.

Too often, the minister safely walks a treadmill of truth that is comfortable for both him and the church. But treadmills tire people out; they don't move them ahead.

> "Like a mighty tortoise,
> Moves the church of God;
> Brethren, we are treading
> Where we've always trod!"

What every minister needs is *prokopē*—pioneer advance into fresh new territory. He needs to study parts of the Bible that he has neglected, and he needs to ask the Lord to teach him lessons that perhaps he has feared. There is no growth without challenge, and there is no challenge without change. The comfortable preacher will rarely be exciting.

An exciting atmosphere

However, it takes more than this to have an exciting message. There must also be in the church family an atmosphere of faith and anticipation, an outlook that says, "Oh, Lord, do a new thing!" As long as the saints are content with business as usual, the pastor will never do his best.

The entire worship service must be saturated with spiritual excitement, it must not be "false fire" manufactured by man, but true spiritual power that can come only from God. The music, the prayers, the reading of the Bible lessons, the Communion, must all give witness that God is present and at work.

Of course, all this must be the result of believing prayer on the part of pastor and people. In many churches, some of the saints gather apart to pray before the services begin; and this is a good practice. Hundreds of people met to pray *while Spurgeon was preaching*, and God's power was manifested in the services.

Jesus compared the Holy Spirit to the wind. We desperately need the "wind of God" to blow upon our lives and throughout our churches! Alas, the air has become stale, and we are no longer breathing the pure oxygen of heaven!

No wonder we announce "services *as usual* next Sunday."

Preacher, let's "stir up the gift of God" and get the fire going! The combination of wind and fire ought to create some excitement!

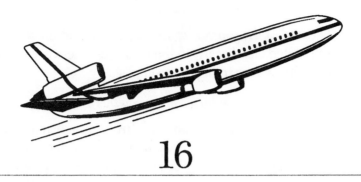

16

Going on a Journey

While the analogy is not perfect, preaching a sermon is something like going on a journey. At least five elements are involved if the journey is to be successful.

1. We must know where we are going.

The preacher who aims at nothing always hits it, but his congregation rarely congratulates him. When asked what we are preaching about, we had better be able to reply with more than the text of the sermon. If we don't know where we are going, we may come to the end of the journey and find ourselves very much alone.

Some preachers are like zany Lord Ronald in Stephen Leacock's story "Gertrude the Governess," who "flung himself upon his horse and rode madly off in all directions." Like the persecuted saints, they go "everywhere preaching the word" (Acts 8:4); only it is the listener, not the preacher, who ends up suffering.

The text must be handled like a map and not like a travel folder. We must do more than present pretty pictures; we must actually seek to take our people to their destination.

The end of the journey must be definite and precise, and it must be stated clearly early in the message; otherwise, nobody will know what we are trying to accomplish.

2. We must know why we are going there.

Behind the stated purpose of the message must be a personal concern, a desire to meet the real needs of our people. If we preach a given text only because it's the next verse in the announced series, or the text given in the lectionary, then we must beware lest we become mechanical ministers instead of loving pastors.

No amount of homiletical skill can compensate for pastoral indifference. The shepherd must know his sheep and seek to help them from the Word. Each message must bring some help and encouragement from the God of all grace, who alone can solve men's problems and give them strength for the burdens of life.

3. We must know how to get there.

A wise traveler plans his journey and tries to find out what he will encounter along the way. Auto clubs provide their members with maps that even point out the speed traps and the construction areas. As we prepare the message, we must anticipate the obstacles we might meet in the minds of our listeners, or the detours that would get us off the main road.

Paul affirms that God is not the author of confusion. The unprepared pastor who credits the Holy Spirit with the disorganized rambling that he calls a sermon is certainly treading on dangerous ground. Reading the map is not the same as making the trip, but the map helps us stay on the right road and avoid detours.

After we complete our preliminary outline, we should check it carefully to see that it takes us where we want to go. Everything in the outline that does not contribute to reaching the goal must be eliminated, no matter how clever or interesting it may be.

"It's nearly all a knotless thread!" was the way one parishioner described her pastor's sermons. She just could not get a handle on what he was saying. Far better that we weave a pattern and make it plain enough for all to see, than that we merely "string things along" and hope it comes out well in the end.

4. We must know when we have arrived at the destination.

A well-known preacher was once introduced by a friend as "a man who needs no introduction; what he really needs is a conclusion." In spite of his effectiveness as a minister, the man had poor terminal facilities and preached too long. In fact, at the end of one sermon, another friend said to him, "Would you like to come to our church and give that series?"

Sermons are not usually improved by stretching them. Once you have covered the text and made the truth personal and practical, get out of the way and trust the Spirit of God to continue to work in hearts. In fact, it might surprise the saints if occasionally we stopped early!

5. We must be willing to pay the price.

The noted British preacher, John Henry Jowett, said, "Preaching that costs nothing accomplishes nothing." True, you can travel free *if* you want to hitchhike or hop a passing freight. But if you have a conscience, you are paying a high price for your freedom.

It may be a cliché, but the statement is still true: We preach, not because we have to say something, but because we have something to say. If we are preaching only because it's our job, then we are hirelings and not shepherds.

Our people don't realize the high cost of effective preaching; but the Lord knows the price that we pay, and it is our responsibility to please Him. If we want our ministry to be authentic, a true witness and not just a proclamation, then we must be prepared to sacrifice. Like David, we must not give to the Lord that which costs us nothing (1 Chron. 21:24).

But time and energy given to honest sermon preparation is an investment in the eternal as well as in our own Christian character. It's worth it!

Happy journeying!

17

Preaching in the Present Tense

A father was showing his young son the wonders of the city museum, when the lad spoke up rather loudly and said, "Dad, let's go someplace where the people and animals are real!" They went to the zoo.

A museum is a great place to study the past, and there is nothing wrong with that; but most of us confess that the zoo is far more interesting. When you get tired of looking at the animals, you can always watch the people. After all, that's how the animals are entertained!

Too often, we treat the Bible like a museum and do all of our preaching in the past tense. The sermon is a history lesson instead of an exciting encounter with the living truth. We are guides in a museum, dusting off the artifacts and explaining the exhibits. And while we are lecturing, our people are saying to themselves, "We wish we could go someplace where things are alive and real!"

What will help us start preaching in the present tense?

Identification

In the ministry, it is easy to become isolated. We spend much of our time with Christian people, talking about Christian things. We read books and magazines that focus on ministry, and we devote hours each week to studying an ancient Book. If we are not careful, we will start building invisible walls that isolate us from reality. We stop living today.

We cannot preach in the present tense unless we know what the present day is like and what our people are experiencing. As he made tents and worked in the marketplace, Paul no doubt learned a great deal about how to understand and help people.

There is no substitute for pastoral visitation, for getting with our people and spending the time necessary to get to know them as more than names and offering envelope numbers. The minister who begrudges the time spent out of the study and with his people does not understand how sermons are prepared.

But the pastor must also know the age in which he lives, the mind-set of the people, the trends, the problems. This is not to suggest that we must go where they go and do what they do! But we had better know how they think and what presuppositions they hold. The barriers in men's minds are far more difficult to tear down than the walls of a prison.

Perspective

Let's face it: it is easy for the pastor to live in the past. He reads church history, ancient theology, the biographies of past leaders, the sermons of great preachers; and much of this is a part of the past. If he has a favorite preacher or theologian, he immerses himself in that topic and ends up judging everything contemporary by it.

Spurgeon was a great preacher; but if he were ministering today, I am sure he would adapt his presentation. Pity the congregation whose pastor thinks he must imitate Thomas Manton or D. Martyn Lloyd Jones! Living in the past, even with the "greats," may encourage you to preach in the past tense; so beware.

It isn't a matter of either/or but both/and. We must understand the past in order to be effective in the present. To paraphrase the old Youth for Christ slogan, our sermons must be "geared to the times but anchored to the Rock."

Imagination

Imagination is the ability to take something old and from it make something new. It is penetrating deeper into reality so that we see relationships that we never saw before. There is nothing new under the sun, but there are new ways to understand and apply old truths.

The Bible is a book of symbols, images, parables, and other forms of imaginative literature; and it is impossible to interpret it accurately without a sanctified imagination. As we better understand what the Bible record says, we can better apply it to the needs of people today. This the work of the imagination—building a bridge of truth from an ancient Book to needy hearts today.

Oswald Chambers wrote: "There is a domain of our nature which we as Christians do not cultivate much, viz., the domain of the imagination." And yet the imagination is one of God's creative gifts to us, a gift we can use for preaching in the present tense.

The Holy Spirit

The Holy Spirit of God is not only infinitely original, but He is always contemporary. He is the only Person on earth today who was "there" when all of those Bible events occurred that we preach about! If we let Him, He will help us better understand both yesterday and today. Then we can prepare messages that will be alive with spiritual insight and practical usefulness for today.

When the minister walks in the Spirit, his spiritual senses are alert, no matter what job he might be doing: studying, visiting, handling an interruption, solving a family problem. The Spirit makes certain that our life in the Word and our life in the world are one exciting experience of growing in God's truth.

When that happens, we can hardly wait to tell our people what God has taught us; and we are preaching in the present tense.

18

Wanted: Unction

A prominent preacher was delayed in getting to a meeting. Seeing this, Satan got there first and told the people he was the substitute. He opened the pulpit Bible, read a text, and proceeded to preach.

The scheduled preacher finally arrived, recognized Satan in the pulpit, and was amazed to hear him declaring evangelical truth. After the meeting, he said to the Devil, "Weren't you afraid to preach the truth of God's Word, lest it weaken your own kingdom?"

Satan smiled and replied, "My preaching won't change anybody's life. You see, I can speak the right words, *but I don't have any unction.*"

What is it?

A.W. Tozer used to say, "If God took the Holy Spirit out of the world, most of what the church is doing would go right on, *and very few people would know the difference.*" This applies to our preaching as much as to any other church ministry, and perhaps more.

The rustic preacher was right when he said, "I can't tell you what unction is, but I can sure tell you *when it ain't!*"

Effective preachers of the Word must have *unction*, the power of the Holy Spirit at work in their lives. This unction is necessary, not only for sermon delivery, but also for sermon *preparation*. The Spirit of God wrote the Bible, and He alone can make it living and real to us. How can He bless a sermon that He didn't help us prepare?

Unction makes the difference between a religious lecture and a burning word from heaven. It makes the difference between words that cut and convict, words that bless and heal, and words that are merely uttered to empty space. When we preach with unction, God uses the Word to accomplish great things.

How do we know?

We must learn to distinguish between true unction and mere "human charisma." When the Spirit of God is at work, the message flows out with clarity and vitality. It excites you, and there is a living bond between you and your listeners. God is there and at work!

The flesh is capable of imitating spiritual unction, but the difference is this: human charisma inflates your ego ("I'm really preaching today!"), while divine unction humbles you and enables you to magnify Jesus Christ. After all, the main ministry of the Spirit is to glorify Christ, not the preacher (John 16:14).

Unction does not relieve us from bearing responsibility or exercising control as we declare the Word. "The spirits of prophets are subject to the prophets" (1 Cor. 14:32), and "the fruit of the Spirit is . . . self-control" (Gal. 5:22,23). The Spirit does not work *instead of us*, as though we were robots. He uses our God-given faculties and gifts as we surrender to Him.

Nor does the Spirit give power *in spite of us*, for He always seeks a fit vessel to fill. If we have done our part, God will do His and give us the power that we need to understand and declare His eternal truth.

A sense of helplessness as we face a congregation is often what the Holy Spirit is looking for. In fact, those times when we feel we have failed may be just the times when the Spirit does His greatest work. Unction is not a predictable commodity that we bargain for at the throne of grace. There must always be the element of God's sovereign grace.

Using a Life

Unless the Spirit of God is our constant source of power day after day, we cannot expect any divine enablement when we preach. Power in the pulpit must not be different from power in our home, in pastoral work, or in the church office.

Secret sin, the neglect of prayer and the Word, bad relationships at home or in the church, unbelief, and a desire for praise can all grieve the Spirit and rob us of power. It is a terrible price to pay.

John A. Broadus, the dean of American homileticians, said, "After all our preparation, general and special, for the conduct of public worship and for preaching, our dependence for real success is on the Spirit of God."

Not that any preacher is perfect, but God knows our frame and sees the desires of our heart. We may not always be conscious of all that God is doing in and through our preaching. Moses did not know that his face was aglow, and Samson did not realize that the power of God had departed from him. Our relationship to God's Spirit is serious and sensitive, and we must walk in the fear of God.

Taking inventory

When we find our hearts getting cold and hard, our minds dull, our wills undisciplined and our work without challenge, then it is time to get alone with God and rekindle the flame on the altar (2 Tim. 1:6). The Holy Spirit is more than willing to grant us the unction we desperately need, but He will do it on His terms.

The important thing is that we seek God's power, not for the purpose of ministerial success, but for the purpose of glorifying Jesus Christ and building His church. G. Campbell Morgan made an awesome statement when he said, "God chooses to be helpless apart from cooperation with man."

"And he [Jesus] did not many mighty works there because of their unbelief" (Matt. 13:58).

"According to your faith be it unto you" (Matt. 9:29).

19

Is It Sunday Again?

The next time you awaken on Sunday morning and groan because you feel you are not prepared to preach, take solace from these words from "The Prince of Preachers," Charles Haddon Spurgeon. He had busy weeks, too!

"My discourse on Sabbath mornings is very frequently the gathering up of the thoughts and experiences of the week—a handful of barley which I have gleaned among the sheaves; but I could not thrust upon you this morning the poverty-stricken productions of my own insufferable dullness of brain, weariness of heart, and sickness of spirit during this week, for this were a sure method of making you partners of my misery.

"I have wandered through a wilderness, but I will not scatter handfuls of the hot sand among you. I have traversed the valley of the shadow of death, but I will not repeat the howlings of Apollyon."

He solved his problem by preaching a sermon on Colossians 3:4 and majoring on Jesus Christ and His relationship to the believer. Without apology, Spurgeon told his people that he had nothing new to say; but he hoped the Spirit would make the old truths new to his congregation.

If you don't have a new message to preach, just remind the saints of the "old truths" that are easily ignored. If anybody complains, show him Philippians 3:1—and think of Spurgeon!

20

The Preaching
of the Cross

I t was said of Charles Spurgeon that, no matter what text he chose, he moved as quickly as possible across country to the cross of Jesus Christ. This is a good example for us to follow.

Spurgeon said to his ministerial students: "More and more am I jealous lest any views upon prophecy, church

government, politics, or even systematic theology, should withdraw one of us from glorying in the cross of Christ. Salvation is a theme for which I would enlist every holy tongue."

"Get them in sight of Calvary," said A.J. Gossip in his lectures on preaching. "Pause there . . . hushed and reverent;

enable them to look, to see it, make it real to them, not just an old tale that has lost its wonder and its stab, but a tremendous awful fact."

"Its wonder and its stab"

Calvary is not only the place of atonement; it is also the place of amazement. Are we so familiar with the cross that we no longer pause to wonder and to worship? Are we able to explain Calvary so completely that no mysteries remain?

The wonder of the cross is itself a worthy theme for ministry. In fact, the cross is the theme of heaven's worship (Rev. 5)! The preacher who handles this topic academically, whose heart is not moved by what the Savior did, is not likely to move anybody else.

"There is something infinitely profounder than pathos in the death of Jesus," wrote Oswald Chambers. "There is a mystery we cannot begin to touch."

But there is also the "stab" of the Calvary message. If you have not recently read A.W. Tozer's essay, "The Old Cross and the New," take time to do so. You will find it in his book *Man: The Dwelling Place of God* (Christian Publ.), as well as in *The Best of A.W. Tozer* (Baker).

A comfortable church does not want a cross that stabs and kills, and yet that is exactly what the cross does to those who understand and apply its message. We want Christ to die for us, but we do not want to die with Christ. We linger in Romans 5 and neglect Romans 6 and 7. We rejoice at the message of *substitution*, but we rebel at the truth of *identification*.

A crossless Gospel is a powerless Gospel (Rom. 1:16); and a crossless Christian is a powerless Christian. Paul gloried in the cross (Gal. 6:14), while believers today rejoice because they have escaped the cross!

The whole Bible

The death of the Son of God is a theme that runs like a crimson cord throughout the whole Bible. Whether in type, psalm or prophecy, the suffering Savior is found from Genesis 3:15 to the end of Revelation. (See *The Master Theme of the Bible* by J. Sidlow Baxter, published by Tyndale.)

The theme of "sacrifice" ties all of Scripture together and emphasizes that "salvation is of the Lord." Key Old Testament texts would be: Genesis 3:15; 22; Exodus 12; Leviticus 16; Numbers 22; Psalms 22 and 69; Isaiah 53. When you turn to the New Testament, the references to the cross are many; and don't forget the many "Lamb" passages in the Book of Revelation.

Make it practical

In Scripture, the death of Jesus Christ is not simply an event in history that has great theological meaning. Paul said, "I am crucified with Christ" (Gal. 2:20). The cross was a part of his everyday experience and had a bearing on all that he did.

The New Testament epistles make it clear that the message of the cross is practical. You cannot come to the cross by faith and live just as you please ever after.

It is significant that crucifixion is one death we cannot perform on ourselves. Men may shoot themselves, poison themselves, drown themselves, gas themselves, and hang themselves; but they cannot crucify themselves. All they can do is yield, which is what Romans 6 and Romans 12:1,2 are all about.

A message for the world

If you preach the cross, you must preach world missions; for He died, not for our sins only, but "for the sins of the whole world" (1 John 2:2). Dr. Charles Koller called the cross "the plus sign on the skyline," and indeed it was.

The cross reconciles sinners to God and saved people to one another. The message of the church is one of reconciliation, not condemnation; and the good news of the Gospel is for the whole world. "For God so loved the world . . ." is the clear message of Calvary.

"The preaching of the cross" is much more than preaching *about* the cross. It means bringing the cross to bear upon every doctrine of the Word, every admonition, every promise. It means seeing God's truth through the cross and the empty tomb.

Some Christian missionaries once visited Mahatma Gandhi, and he asked them to sing him one of their hymns. "Which one?" they asked. He replied, "Sing for me the one that best expresses what you are preaching."

It took them but a moment to decide, and together they sang "When I Survey the Wondrous Cross."

They made the right choice.

Think on these things

- Jesus was crucified, not in a cathedral between two candles, but on a cross between two thieves.   —*George F. MacLeod*

- The cross cannot be defeated, for it is defeat.
  —*Gilbert K. Chesterton*

- There are no crown-wearers in heaven who were not cross-bearers here below.   —*Charles Haddon Spurgeon*

- We need men of the cross, with the message of the cross, bearing the marks of the cross.   —*Vance Havner*

- Christ's cross is such a burden as sails are to a ship or wings to a bird.   —*Samuel Rutherford*

- He came to pay a debt He didn't owe because we owed a debt we couldn't pay.   —*Anonymous*

- The old cross slew men; the new cross entertains them. The old cross condemned; the new cross amuses. The old cross destroyed confidence in the flesh; the new cross encourages it.   —*A.W. Tozer*

- All heaven is interested in the cross of Christ, all hell is terribly afraid of it, while men are the only beings who more or less ignore its meaning.   —*Oswald Chambers*

- The cross: God's way of uniting suffering with love.
  —*Georgia Harkness*

- The figure of the Crucified invalidates all thought which takes success for its standard.   —*Dietrich Bonhoeffer*

- The cross is God's plus sign to a needy world. —*Anonymous*

- The cross is the only ladder high enough to reach heaven's threshold.   —*G.D. Boardman*

21

Pick a Preacher, Any Preacher

P ainters study the lives and works of other painters, and musicians do the same with musicians; but for some reason, preachers ignore their own heritage.

For years, I have been encouraging my fellow preachers to "dig again the old wells" and get acquainted with the lives and preaching of the pulpit giants. I am enthusiastic about this matter, because "meeting" the pulpit giants has greatly enriched my own life and ministry, and I would wish this same blessing for others.

Perspective and passion

I once taught a seminary course on the history of preaching. My goal was twofold: perspective and passion. We need perspective in order to realize that *our* way of preaching is not the only way and that God uses a variety of people to build His church. If you know this, it will save you from both pride and discouragement.

But I was hoping, too, that as a result of the course, each student would "fall in love" with one of the giants and make him a "homiletical hero" for life. I suggest that you do the same, because a passion for a great preacher can help you discover and develop your own skills.

This is not to suggest that we imitate our hero. God forbid! We must heed the counsel that Alexander Whyte gave to his young assistant who gave a sermon that "sounded" like Whyte: "Sir, preach your own message!"

Nor am I suggesting that we select a preacher like ourselves, in style or even in theology. We might benefit more by studying a man whose ministry is much different from ours—somebody who will be a window, not a mirror. Through one man's life and work, you can get insight into a whole period in history. This can give you tremendous help for your ministry today.

Have a hero

In my own case, there have been at least three heroes over the course of more than forty years of ministry. The first is G. Campbell Morgan (who went Home on the day I was celebrating my sixteenth birthday), then Frederick W. Robertson of Bristol, and finally Phillips Brooks, the famous Boston preacher.

The best way to "pick a preacher" is to read widely and get acquainted with many of them. Browse through *20 Centuries of Great Preaching*, a most valuable set for the serious minister of the Word. Perhaps a certain era in church history attracts you, or a certain doctrinal emphasis. Read the sermons of many men and see how you respond to them. (Warning: Don't make any final rejections. Some men you have to "grow into.")

Having been a Sherlock Holmes fan from childhood, I have a great love for the Victorian era in England; and I have made the preachers of that era my focus of interest. You may prefer the Reformation period, or the days of the Puritans, or the era of the church fathers. But be sure the choice is yours and is meaningful to you, no matter what any of the "experts" might say.

Once you have selected your hero, start to read the best biographies about him—any autobiographies that may be available—and, of course, as many of his published sermons as you can find. Turn to the history books and study the era in which he lived. How did events in history affect him and what he preached?

Are there books about his approach to preaching? Did he deliver any lectures on preaching? What did others say about his ministry? What lasting contributions did he make to the field of homiletics? There are many possibilities, once you get started.

Read the man's sermons, first, as a *sinner* needing the message of God's grace, but then as a *student* who wants to learn better how to study and preach the Word of God. There is an excellent work sheet on "How to Study a Sermon" in *The Protestant Pulpit*, edited by Andrew Blackwood.

Good biographics must be read many times before the subject becomes real to you. Likewise, a good sermon must be read and pondered again and again. The day will come when you will begin to "see" and "hear" the preacher in the sermon, and then you know you are really starting to penetrate his mind and heart. Stay with it!

The busy preacher certainly cannot devote many hours a week to this kind of study, but it can be a healthy diversion that both refreshes and enriches. Carry a book with you and take advantage of those extra minutes that come your way each day.

There is something inspirational about the influence of a great life. But even more, there is something rich and rewarding for our ministries when we "walk with the giants" and let them teach us what God has taught them.

It is no secret that Charles Spurgeon admired George Whitefield and patterned himself after him. Dr. D. Martyn Lloyd-

Jones was also an admirer of Whitefield. Alexander Whyte saturated himself with the writings of the Puritan preacher, Thomas Goodwin. The "giants" gladly acknowledged their debt to other "giants"!

Elbert Hubbard said, "Biography broadens the vision and allows us to live a thousand lives in one."

We may not get acquainted with a thousand preachers, but we ought to get acquainted with at least one who excites and encourages us to do our best.

22

Preaching from Proverbs

Perhaps it is time to give your people a diet of God's holy wisdom as revealed in the Book of Proverbs. But beware! If you don't take time to prepare—and that includes getting a grasp of how to interpret the book—you may find yourself merely giving a series of moral lectures based on isolated texts. That is not preaching God's Word!

Derek Kidner's fine commentary on Proverbs in the Tyndale Old Testament series (IVP) is a good place to start. The introductory material, including the "subject studies," is very important if you want to interpret Proverbs with accuracy. Also, consult the articles on "Hebrew wisdom literature" in the Bible encyclopedias and the Old Testament introductions.

The people in Proverbs

But, what kind of series shall we plan? One approach is to deal with the *people* in Proverbs: the wise man, the fool (and there are several kinds in Proverbs), the sluggard, and so on.

This can be topical preaching that really meets the needs of the people.

A second approach is to tie a key text to important Bible people. For instance, Proverbs 28:13 can apply to David; Proverbs 27:6 to Judas; Proverbs 15:8 to King Saul, and so on. The text then becomes the key to the person's life.

Let others choose

In fact, you can ask your church family to read Proverbs (a chapter a day for a month) and select verses that they think apply to different men and women in the Bible. You may not use all of their choices, but what they choose will make you think!

You may want to consult some of these books, along with the standard commentaries: *Studies in Proverbs* by William Arnot (Kregel); *The Book of Proverbs* by David Thomas (Kregel); *An Exposition of Proverbs* by Charles R. Bridges (Zondervan); *Proverbs* by H.A. Ironside (Loizeaux). *Self Control* by Russell Kelfer (Tyndale) is a topical study that focuses on the need for personal discipline.

Finally, check the sermons of the great preachers. Joseph Parker has some illuminating material in his *People's Bible* volume on Proverbs, and there are forty-three messages from Proverbs in Spurgeon's printed sermons. It helps to see how other preachers have handled this part of God's Holy Word.

23

Let Us Begin

I have no statistical proof, but I believe that at least 50 percent of the sermons preached last Sunday started with "Now, if you have your Bibles, please turn to. . . ." The other 50 percent began with "Now, you'll remember that last week we discussed. . . ."

Of course, many preachers feel that this is the best way to start each sermon. After all, these statements are familiar, so nobody has to pay attention. And they give the people opportunity to put down the hymnal (or the baby), pick up the Bible and locate the text. It also gives the minister time to get his notes together and his brain settled in the pulpit, especially if he's the kind who needs to rev up the motors before he can take off.

But even these advantages don't make this kind of introduction the best way to start a sermon. If the sermon text is in the worship folder ("bulletin" to the nonliturgical), the congregation can be prepared when the sermon starts: Bible open, eyes on the preacher, ears and hearts open to God's truth. The minister ought to be ready to preach the moment he gets behind the pulpit, so why waste time on a pointless opening statement? If he needs to get things together, let him pause for a brief prayer.

97

Why an introduction anyway?

The older books on homiletics described many types of introductions and explained when to use them. They gave us numerous reasons why our sermons needed introductions: to set the atmosphere, to announce the theme, to give the context of the Bible text, to break down barriers and so on.

But in this age of fast-food, digests and "get away vacations," we had better think twice before we plan a long introduction for the message, at least as far as our regular church congregation is concerned. They know us, they are there to listen to us, and they don't want to be kept on the runway. Let's take off!

The main purpose of the sermon introduction is to tell them what we are preaching about and why they need to listen. *Content* and *intent*—that's what introductions are all about.

Both factors are important, and both must be given concisely. A long, rambling introduction, with numerous flashbacks to previous sermons, will only confuse the visitors, bore the regulars and encourage both groups to turn us off until something really interesting starts to happen.

The worshiper is asking us two questions: "What are you preaching about?" and "Why should I listen?" The sooner we answer, the better off all of us will be.

Wanted: Precision

If doctors were as vague in their prescriptions as some preachers are in their theme statements, most of us would be dead. Determining that "propositional statement," and fine-tuning it to say precisely what ought to be said, challenges even the most seasoned preacher of the Word.

When you read the sermons of the "greats" of the past, you notice that most of them have long introductions. (In fact, the farther back you go, the longer they get!) But you must remember that their people had nothing exciting to do at home, and they expected the "pulpit discourse" to be long and heavy. Not so today. People want us to get to the point as soon as possible. For example:

"People don't really believe the story of the Prodigal Son these days. Most of the prodigals we know, or we hear about in the news, never seem to get into trouble. Instead of ending up in the pigpen, they seem to end up on top of the world! How do you explain this? If it doesn't pay to be good, why be good?"

Or: "All of us know that we should pray. Prayer is important to the Christian, to the Christian home, and to the church. Why is prayer so difficult for us? What can we do to make prayer really a vital part of our lives?"

Either of these introductions will get the listeners' attention, tell them why they should listen and lead right into a sermon statement.

If the context of a passage is important to the message, then work it in early in the first point; but try to keep the introduction from becoming a survey of Bible history or a review of your last three sermons. To keep from digressing, write out the introduction and stick to it.

When an introduction grows long and complicated, it's usually a sign that something is wrong with the sermon statement (proposition) or that we are attempting to cover too much ground. Sharpen the focus of the message and your troubles will end.

Something arresting and convincing happens when a pastor steps into the pulpit *and immediately starts to preach*. In Bible conference ministry, I have noticed that many speakers who "stroll into" their messages lose the congregation after a few minutes. *If the listeners are in earnest to hear, we ought to be in earnest to preach.*

This is not to suggest that the introduction be so abrupt that it catches people by surprise and leaves them behind. Lyman Abbott said in his *Yale Lectures*, "As to introductions, generally the less introduction the better. . . . He who strikes the heart of his subject in the first sentence is the one most likely to secure an attentive listening at the outset of his discourse."

Yes, some occasions will call for a different approach; and wise is the pastor who knows his occasions.

An anonymous prayer

> From the cowardice that shrinks from new truth,
> From the laziness that is content with half-truths,
> From the arrogance that thinks it knows all truth,
> O God of truth, deliver us!

24

A Sin in Good Standing

"Why did you preach my pastor's sermon last night?" a student asked me at a seminary Bible conference.

"I'm not sure I know your pastor," I replied, "and I rarely get to hear other men preach. Was I in the congregation when you heard him preach it?"

"No, I guess you weren't," he mumbled. "Maybe you just preach alike." And with that, he walked away. I was glad to close the conversation, because I might have been tempted to tell him that the message had been in print for several years and was also available on tape. I certainly didn't want to undermine his faith in his pastor.

Perhaps his pastor did happen to hit upon the same outline and illustrations that I used. Perhaps we do "preach alike." Perhaps . . . but I must confess that I had a strong feeling that Pastor X was guilty of "a sin in good standing" in the ministry—plagiarism.

Stealing?

Of course, we all joke about it and argue, "If you steal from one author, it's plagiarism; but if you steal from many, it's research." Of course, we don't really "steal"—we "borrow." And we hope that the people who listen to us don't know where our material came from.

You may have heard about the pastor who was preaching his way through a book of sermons written by a famous preacher; but, unknown to him, a man in his congregation owned the same book.

"Excellent sermon, Pastor!" the man said as he left church one Sunday.

"Thank you!" smiled the minister.

"Next week's is good, too!" added the man; and with that Parthian shot, he left the pastor in confusion.

Very few preachers are original; all of us are midgets standing on the shoulders of giants. "The ancients have stolen all our best thoughts!" is our constant complaint. So much good sermonic material is available these days (you can even subscribe to "sermon services," but we don't recommend it) that it is easy for the preacher to coast in his studies and feed his people on borrowed, secondhand bread.

Dishonesty?

The first person to suffer, however, is not the parishioner; it is the pastor. Something happens to the character of the minister who is dishonest in his preaching. It is simply impossible to preach the truth and at the same time live a lie.

Our messages ought to grow out of our personal walk with the Lord and our ministry to our people. Of course, we will read and study everything that can help us; but the final product must be our own. As a friend of mine likes to put it, "I milk a lot of cows, but I make my own butter!"

There is certainly nothing wrong with using another man's material, provided we sincerely give credit. The word *plagiarize* comes from a Latin word that means "to kidnap," and kidnaping is a serious offense. But the law permits us to *entertain* the "brain children" of others. We might even "reclothe" them in our own way, but let's not claim paternity.

Blessed is that preacher who reads widely and who recognizes excellence when he meets it. Even more blessed is that preacher who can enrich his own ministry without robbing others, but who can use what he finds in an honest way, to the good of his people and to the glory of God.

P.S. When tempted to plagiarize, meditate on 1 Chronicles 21:24.

Plagiarism

* Stealing a ride on someone else's train of thought.
  —*Russell E. Curran*

* Borrowing, if it be not bettered by the borrower.
  —*John Milton*

* Taking something from one man and making it worse.
  —*George Moore*

* The highest form of compliment and the lowest form of larceny.   —*Anon.*

* Plagiarist: an educated pickpocket and a literary body-snatcher.   —*Anon.*

* When people are free to do as they please, they usually imitate each other.   —*Eric Hoffer*

25

What Was He Talking About?

C alvin Coolidge, who never wasted words, came home
from church and was asked by his wife, "What did the
preacher preach about?"

"Sin," replied the President in his usual laconic fashion.

"Well, what did he say about it?"

"He was against it."

At least Mr. Coolidge *knew* what his pastor was preaching
about. Not everybody who attends church is that fortunate.

Vagueness in a sermon is an unpardonable sin, like
vagueness in a medical prescription or on a map. To quote
Ruskin, a preacher has "thirty minutes to raise the dead," and
the miracle does not usually take place when the message is
unclear and the preacher is uncertain where he is going.

Complexity is not the same thing as profundity. Insurance
policies are certainly complex, but there is nothing profound
about them. Compared to some sermons, an insurance policy is
a child's primer. Our Lord was simple in His teaching and yet
very profound, for true profundity comes from simplicity.

How, then, can we avoid vagueness in our teaching and preaching?

1. *We must have a definite aim for every message and state that aim in a direct and simple sentence.* Our people should be able to stop us before the service and ask, "In one sentence, Pastor, what are you talking about today?"—and expect a clear and ready answer.

The statement might be a simple sentence: "Our Lord gives us four instructions to follow in winning the war against worry." Or, it might be a question: "How, then, do we win the war against worry?" If you feel up to it, you can even dare to make it an exhortation: "Let's win the war against worry!"

Finding that precise statement is one of the hardest parts of sermon preparation, but hard studying on our part leads to easier listening on the part of the people.

2. *We must use concrete terms and not abstractions, being careful to define the important words.* If your message is about freedom, tell us what the word means; because each of us has a different and probably very vague idea of what freedom is. Use your dictionary of synonyms to get that precise definition; and then make that definition "alive" to your listeners. Often a good quotation will do the job.

Abstractions become obstructions apart from illustrations. In the Sermon on the Mount, Jesus did not discuss the Hebrew and Greek words for worry. Instead, He talked about birds and lilies and burglaries.

Most Hebrew and Greek words have fascinating pictures within them, so don't turn them into bewildering theological terms. *Redemption* moves you into the slave market, *justification* into the court room, *departure* into the army camp, and so on. There are many excellent linguistic tools available today to help you better understand the divine vocabulary.

3. *We must cite specific facts and avoid generalities.* "You

will recall the American Airlines crash at O'Hare Field on May 25, 1979, that took the lives of 274 people" carries a lot more power than, "That plane crash a few years ago—I forget the name of the airline—it was O'Hare Field and hundreds of people died."

Specific and accurate facts not only give a stronger impact to the message, but they also quietly convey the fact that you cared enough to do your homework.

One of the handiest books for checking current facts is the humble almanac. The encyclopedia annual is an excellent resource for current biographical facts. If you want to build your credibility and get a reputation for accuracy, take time to get the facts.

4. *We must always apply the Word in a practical way.* One of the best ways to test the clarity of a sermon is to go over it point by point and courageously ask yourself, "So what? What difference would it make if I left this out?"

Clear preaching begins with clear thinking, and clear thinking involves determining what you want the message to do in the lives of the people. If your applications are vague, it may be that your interpretation of the Word, or the organization of the message, are lacking clarity. If we know what we are talking about, we can always say "Therefore . . ."

5. *We must relate every doctrine to Jesus Christ.* The Word must become flesh. When Paul wanted to get a generous missions offering from the Corinthians, he reminded them of "the grace of our Lord Jesus Christ" (2 Cor. 8:9). When he wanted to urge husbands to love their wives, he told them about Christ's love for the church (see Eph. 5:25ff). This is what it means to "preach Christ" and to do it effectively.

We don't want our people leaving church and asking, "What was he aiming at?" No, we want them to say, "Did not our heart burn within us?" And we want them to come back for more.

26

The Enemies of Preaching

No, this is not a tirade against the world, the flesh and the Devil, although, if they are influencing your life, they can damage a good sermon in no time. My great concern is that we learn to recognize the *hidden* enemies of good preaching, enemies that constantly lurk around us in the study, in the sanctuary—and even in the prayer closet.

Greatness

The first of these enemies is the preacher's obsession with preaching "great sermons." Like the baseball player who keeps trying for home runs, when what is really needed is a man on first, this preacher struggles week by week to knock the ball out of the park and never quite makes it. High ideals are important in pulpit ministry, but sometimes the best is the enemy of the good.

"The notion of a great sermon, either constantly or occasionally haunting the preacher, is fatal," said Phillips Brooks in his *Yale Lectures on Preaching*. "The sermons of which nobody speaks . . . are the sermons that do the work, that make men better men, and really sink into their affections."

To change the image, the cook does not prepare a Thanksgiving feast for every meal. A good cook just makes sure that there is nourishing, tasty food on the table each time the diners gather.

Compliments

The compliments of our kind and patient people can easily become an enemy to good preaching, especially if we believe them. To be sure, there are listeners in every congregation who would compliment us no matter what we said or how we said it. This routine chatter we learn to recognize and ignore. But when we get sincere appreciation from people whom we consider to be discerning listeners, that is another story. We then say to ourselves, "I didn't work too hard on that one, and yet they liked it!" Then the trap falls and we start to get careless in our preparation.

Not that we don't appreciate their kind words! We do, and we wish we would merit them more often. But good preaching cannot be tied to what our people have to say about us. After all, they could be wrong; and in the final judgment, it is what the Lord thinks about our ministry that really counts. One sermon does not make a ministry.

How often we have gone home after a service, convinced that the sermon was a failure, only to learn during the weeks that followed that the Lord used the message, poor as it was, to help several people. On the other hand, many of the "home runs" turned out to be foul balls, at least from the human standpoint. His Word never returns void, we know, but there are times when it takes a lot of faith to believe that.

Statistics

Another insidious enemy is that snare of statistics. Perhaps church attendance is on the increase, lost sinners are being converted, and people are uniting with the church. Certainly this kind of "success" must prove that our preaching is drawing men and women to Christ and the local fellowship. We have arrived!

Perhaps. Except that nobody can really be sure *why* anybody attends church or why they make "spiritual decisions." We like to think that these blessings come because the Holy Spirit uses our sermons, but we will not know for sure until the books are opened. Our pulpit ministry may have little or nothing to do with the increase or decrease in statistics. It may be the music that draws the people, or perhaps the children's program or the "social status" of the members.

We dare not measure the quality of our sermons by the quantity of the statistics. If we do, we might become either too elated or too depressed; and both pride and discouragement are sins. One day our Lord gave a sermon on the Bread of Life and lost His whole congregation; and yet false prophets always seem to have a crowd.

Imitation

One of the most dangerous enemies of preaching is the imitating of some preacher we admire. Every minister has a shelf of "homiletical household gods" to which he gives secret homage, such as G. Campbell Morgan, R.G. Lee, Charles Haddon Spurgeon or perhaps some popular contemporary media minister whose sermons stir him. Since we all tend to become like the idols we worship (Psalm 115:8), a certain amount of imitation is inevitable.

I recall a preacher who was so enamored of G. Campbell Morgan that he often said in his sermons, "O, my masters!" as

Morgan used to do. His listeners could never quite figure out what he was talking about or who those "masters" were. Fortunately, he saw his folly and stopped imitating Morgan. It's good to have homiletical heroes, but be sure you imitate the essentials in their ministry and not the accidentals.

An ax to grind

Here is another enemy: when the preacher has "an ax to grind," the sermon is headed for the slaughter. Many congregations wait anxiously for the first sermon after the monthly board meeting, knowing that the pastor will either consciously or unconsciously tell them how the meeting went. It is tragic when a man of God hides behind the pulpit and attacks people who have no way to fight back—until the next board meeting.

Suddenness

One last enemy must be mentioned: suddenness. Charles Spurgeon said, "Suddenness leads to shallowness"; and he was right. Sermons are not manufactured, they grow; and they cannot grow unless we give them time to grow. We don't "build" sermons the way little boys build model airplanes. We nurture them; and that means taking time to meditate, pray and cultivate the seed of the Word planted in our hearts.

Yes, there are times when the days are too short and the schedule is too long. Yes, there are weeks when the pastoral demands take us out of the study more than we would like. God knows all about this and graciously compensates for it, *if we have been faithful all the other times*. Often it is while we are out shepherding in the field that God sends us the very message we had groped for in the study.

I am told that the Great Wall of China was penetrated at least three times in history, and each time the enemy bribed one of the guards. All of the resources of heaven are behind the faithful preacher of the Word, so we have nothing to fear—except the enemies who bribe us and get in because we let them.

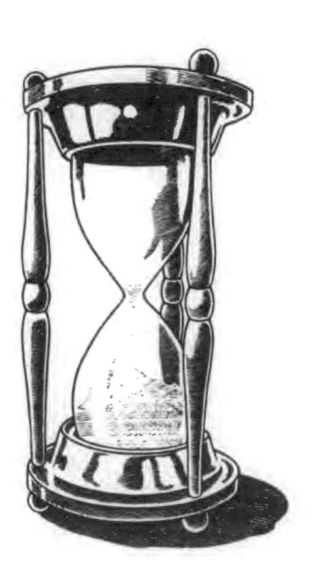

27

If I Only Had Time!

I f you find yourself saying in your sermons, "Now, if I had
the time—" then beware! A pastor I know frequently
punctuated his sermons with "If I had the time," and one
Sunday a deacon approached him about it.

"Pastor, you keep saying 'If I had the time.' *Why* don't you
have the time? *You* prepare the sermon and *you* plan the service,
so you have nobody to blame but yourself."

He paused a moment and then added: "I'll bet if we started
the service fifteen minutes earlier, it wouldn't make a bit of
difference."

Well, the deacon may have been a bit blunt and brutal,
but he got his point across; and it is a point that we need to take
to heart. *Never complain about the time; it only wastes more
time and keeps you from using the time you have to best
advantage.* Furthermore, it calls attention to the time, and that
is something a good preacher does not want to do!

If in the pulpit you find yourself like the mummy, "pressed

115

for time," then you are ready for a pastoral inventorv. Be honest, now! Are you wasting time?

Our people come to worship God, and we must never look upon what occurs prior to the sermon as "preliminaries," matters that we can adjust at will. Preaching should be an act of worship just as much as the singing or the giving. Hearing the message is an act of worship on the part of the people.

Balance

An effective worship service must have balance, and wise is the pastor who knows how to keep the elements of worship from competing with each other. Each week, decide how much time each element needs, and stick to your limits. That includes the sermon!

Beware of the time-wasters; starting the service late; preaching the announcements; too much spontaneous chatter in between the parts of the service; taking too long to introduce the sermon. Why read the bulletin to the people and rob them of the privilege of reading it for themselves?

Now, let's think about that sermon. Are you trying to cover too much territory? Is the Scripture text too long or the sermon topic too broad? All Scripture is inspired and profitable, but we don't have to cover it all in one message.

Distillation

Have you distilled the message into that crystal clear sentence that announces the content and the intent of the sermon? Have you really spent time thinking the message through and sharpening its focus? Younger preachers in particular have a tendency to try to say too much. Use your wastebasket or file away the unused ideas for future use.

One day I complained to a friend about my busy schedule, and he quietly replied, "There is always time for the will of

God." He was right—and there is always time for the *message of God,* *if* we are listening to Him and preparing His Word with care. Find out what God wants you to say in the sermon and plan to say it in the time God gives you.

Carelessness

Preachers who do expository series are sometimes guilty of careless planning. They hope to cover Romans 5:1-5; but, if they don't, they can always "pick it up" next week. Shame on them! They either did not know what God's message was for that day, or they did not prepare it carefully.

This is not to deny that God can break in and "expand" a sermon so that the pastor says more than he intended to say. But when that happens, everybody will know it and nobody will complain. It is the week-after-week "leftovers" that disturb the congregation. They wonder if their pastor knows where he is going.

Sermonic surgery

Even while we are preaching the message, it is good to "weigh" the points and decide if we need to leave some things out. Better not to mention them at all than to drag the items in and not be able to deal with them. Blessed is that preacher who has a sense of balance and timing and who knows how to perform even last-minute surgery on the sermon when necessary!

Time is the table on which we set the spiritual meal for our church family. Don't attempt to put a ten-course meal on a game table—unless you are a good juggler or you don't mind leaving a mess behind! If you are concerned about eternity, you will make wise use of time.

28

What's What About Who's Who

B iographical preaching is perhaps the most rewarding, and yet the most difficult, kind of pulpit ministry. The Bible is a *Who's Who* of people who met God, knew God, trusted God, and either glorified Him or grieved Him.

People identify with people. The men and women found in the Bible are just like the men and women in our homes and churches today. Anybody can meet himself or herself in the Bible.

How do you go about preaching a series on the life of a great Bible character, or perhaps on several of the men and women of Scripture? Here are a few suggestions.

1. *Get to know the person intimately by studying all the relevant data in Scripture.* Immerse yourself in the biblical record. Don't forget that the New Testament has something to say about some of the Old Testament worthies. Alexander Whyte's *Bible Characters from the Old and New Testaments* (Kregel) will help you in this area.

2. *Understand the historical setting.* The best commentaries and encyclopedias will assist you here, and be sure to note the bibliographies for specialized studies.

3. *As you get to know the person, look for a "key truth" in his or her life.* Not every preacher will choose the same key idea, of course; but try to "build" the character's life around one main truth. With Barnabas it could well be *encouragement*; with Jonah it might be *prejudice*. George Matheson's volumes on *Portraits of Bible Men and Women* (Kregel) have been most helpful to me when it comes to pinpointing a key idea in a person's life.

4. *Determine how many messages you can preach and still say something.* You could spend a year on the life of David, but it might get boring both to you and your congregation. Why touch on every detail? Hit the highlights and seek to maintain the interest of the people. In short, don't try to cover too much material.

5. *Remember that you are preaching sermons—you have a personal object in view for each message; you are not giving lectures on biography, archaeology or history.* The purpose of preaching is not just to explain a subject; you also want to achieve an object. You want to help the people in their daily lives. Keep each message personal and practical.

6. *It's wise to block out the whole series well in advance, even though you may not outline each message.* Know where you are going, and seek to tie each message together by some general theme.

7. *Relate each message to Christ. Preach Christ and what He alone can do for the human heart.* Many Old Testament personalities beautifully illustrate New Testament doctrines.

The standard set for biographical study is Hastings' *Greater Men and Women of the Bible*. I get helpful insights from Alexander Whyte's set of *Bible Characters*, now available in one volume. Clovis Chappell and Clarence Macartney both have fine books of sermons on Bible characters. F.B. Meyer's books on Bible personalities are too well known to be listed here. They are helpful.

A different approach to biographical studies is Frederick Buechner's *Peculiar Treasures* (Harper & Row). It contains about 125 vignettes of Bible personalities, all of them from a new perspective. Buechner is really "off the wall" in some of his studies, but he is still interesting and stimulating.

Of course, there are many biographical studies on the key people of Scripture—David, Abraham, Paul, Peter, and so on. Don't forget G. Campbell Morgan's excellent *The Great Physician* (Revell), and Herbert Lockyer's many volumes on the men, women, kings and queens of the Bible. *Personalities Around Paul* by D. Edmond Hiebert (Moody Press) is very useful if you plan a biographical series from Acts and the epistles. *The Companions of St. Paul* by John S. Howson is an older work; you may find it in a used-book store. Theodore Epp's biographical studies are a treasury of spiritual truth.

In recent months, I have been getting acquainted with Jeremiah, and it has been a thrilling experience. What a man! And what a challenge his life is to us today!

That's what biographical preaching is all about—turning old portraits into modern "moving pictures" and making dead people live and great truths come alive to help us serve God better today.

29

Let's Polish the Pulpit

As preachers of the Word, our basic tool is *language*. What tools are to a mechanic, *words* are to a minister. If the mechanic or carpenter needs to be skilled in the use of his tools, certainly the preacher needs to be skilled in the use of words.

The time has come for us to polish the pulpit and do a better job of putting words together as we seek to share the precious truths of God's Word.

Clear preaching begins with clear thinking. No amount of clever vocabulary can atone for fuzzy thinking. If the preacher doesn't know what he is talking about, neither will anybody else.

This means that the propositional statement for each sermon must be accurate, precise and clear. "I just want to share a few thoughts about the atonement" is an invitation to a homiletical disaster. "Because Jesus Christ has died for us, we have four exciting privileges" will probably get their attention and hold it.

Things to avoid

We preachers should avoid using the word "things" when a more precise word could do the job better. (I know, Paul uses "things" repeatedly in Romans 8, but he was an inspired apostle.) Many of my esteemed British ministerial heroes used "things" and seemed to get away with it, but I personally try to avoid it. "This psalm reveals several things about the Christian life" is, to me, very weak. What's wrong with, "In this psalm, God reveals five wonderful resources that we have as believers in Jesus Christ"?

That key word needs to be precise, so use your dictionary of synonyms. There is a difference between "results" and "consequences."

Vocabulary

Another area that needs polishing is the preacher's general vocabulary. Unless you are a converted gangster, try to avoid words like "guys," "dopes" and other expressions that only cheapen the pulpit. "Children" is preferred to "kids" and "courage" is much better than "guts."

It is remarkable how many preachers do not know English grammar and use "for you and I" and other unpardonable expressions. Try preaching in shorter sentences; it will help you stay out of grammatical and syntactical mazes. Direct and simple speech accomplishes much more than tangled oratory.

Grammar and clichés

If a minister has a problem with grammar, he might ask a capable member of his congregation to tell him when he has erred. Early in his ministry, Charles Spurgeon had such a critic (the writer was anonymous); and the great preacher admitted that the weekly postcard was a big help to him in polishing his preaching.

While we are at it, let's avoid the clichés that make the

rounds—such meaningless phrases as "point in time" and "let's plug into it." Add to the clichés your list of favorite "journalese" phrases that are useless because they cloud meanings instead of radiating light and truth.

I wish every preacher, serious about words, would read Edwin Newman's *A Civil Tongue* and *Strictly Speaking*. The books by William Safire are also helpful: *On Language, What's the Good Word?* and *I Stand Corrected*.

Be yourself

I am not pleading for artificial language or an academic vocabulary. Be yourself, but be your *best* self. Words are tools, yes, they are even weapons; and we want to know how to use them the best way possible.

What Erasmus wrote of his friend, Colet, ought to be true of us as the preachers of God's truth:

"You say what you mean, and you mean what you say. Your words have birth in your heart, not on your lips. They follow your thoughts instead of your thoughts being shaped by them. You have the happy art of expressing with ease what others can hardly express with the greatest labor."

We have not yet arrived—but is anything hindering us from starting?

30

When the Message Doesn't Come

Here it is, Friday afternoon, and you aren't ready for Sunday. It's been one of those weeks. You've had a lot them lately ... always busy, and yet seemingly no time for sermon preparation.

When you have a series of "futile Fridays," you can be sure that something has probably gone wrong with your priorities. Granted, there are occasional emergencies that so mangle your schedule that even the finest administrator couldn't rescue it. But when *every* Friday finds you sermonless, it's time to ask, "Is preaching really important to me?"

Study

A pastor must do many things, but at the hub of them is studying and proclaiming the Word of God. Everything else contributes to that—the pastoral visits (so he can preach to the needs of real people), the administration (so the wheels run smoothly and people exercise their gifts), the time off (so his mind and body are fit instruments for service), the hours of study (so he has something to say).

I know, the ministry has a built-in dilemma that nobody completely solves. The more we study and prepare, the better we preach. And the better we preach, the more our people ask to see us so they can share their needs. But the more people we see, the less time we have for preparation! Alas!

Counseling

One answer is to be more selective in your counseling. There are people in your church family who can handle many of the routine problems that people bring to you, and you ought to permit them to exercise their gifts. I'm not suggesting "passing the buck" or giving counselees the impression that you don't care. Rather, it's a matter of openness, tact and a lot of courage.

Try not to counsel people who don't come to hear you preach. You may end up meeting with all the malcontents in town, people who ought to talk with their own pastors. If they will give God's Word a chance, it can meet their needs.

But, back to that unfinished sermon. We can't change the past (even if we do make promises for the future), and you *do* have to preach on Sunday. What should you do?

Points to ponder

1. Maybe you need to get away for some "ventilation." You can't do good creative work under pressure. Sometimes we're so close to our work, we lose perspective. If you have been planting the seed in the soil of your soul, maybe a couple of hours' walk in the park, some window-shopping, or a visit to a quiet spot for reflection, will help get the creative juices flowing again, Do something different!

2. Check your exegesis. Have you really grasped the message of the text? Or have you forced on the text some clever idea of your own?

3. Read the passage again and again in several translations. Read it out loud. Listen to what it says.

4. Start preaching the sermon to yourself or writing it in your typewriter or computer, and see what develops. Many creative people get their best ideas by just "diving in" and getting underway.

5. Maybe your purposes are confused or unclear; or maybe you're trying to cover too much in one message. What do you want to accomplish? How does the text help you accomplish it? Can you summarize the thrust of the message in a clear sentence? If not, then stay at your desk until you can.

6. Read a couple of good sermons on the same text—but don't borrow them!

7. As a last resort, "talk your way" through the message with a fellow-pastor or other confidential friend. Maybe two hearts and minds, meeting together, will generate some sparks and start a homiletical fire.

For years, I've been telling pastors to work two weeks in advance in their basic preparation. Of course, you make the final outline for the message a few days before you preach it; but you do your "spadework" in advance. If you have a guest speaker, don't take the week off. Use it to get ahead; and, if the speaker has to cancel (this has happened to me!), you will be prepared.

Real preaching is hard work, and it deserves the best we can give it. We must learn to say "No" to a lot of trivial things so that we might have a resounding "Yes!" when we step into the pulpit.

31

Playing David's Harp

B lessed is that congregation whose minister knows how to preach nourishing messages from the Psalms. To be pitied is that church whose pastor is an inveterate analyzer, who uses his kit of homiletical scalpels on these marvelous poems and ends up performing autopsies instead of preparing meals.

All of which means that if you want to succeed in preaching the Psalms, you must have the right mind-set as you prepare. While careful analysis is necessary when you study any portion of Scripture, especially Paul's theological arguments, it may not be your most important tool as you sing and sob with David or Asaph. Perhaps your greatest asset is an open and an honest heart that can identify in some measure with the feelings expressed in the song.

This is not to say that we must never analyze or outline a psalm. Some of the psalms lend themselves beautifully to outlining (Psalm 19, for example), but a homiletical analysis is not the

major goal as you study. When you study the Psalms, use your
spiritual stethoscope before you use your X-ray machine. Feel
the heartbeat of the writer. Enter into his joys and sorrows, his
prayers and praises; and see how his experiences with God relate
to your own life today. Meet yourself in the Psalms.

"We should never lay aside the Book of Psalms," said
Luther, "but should constantly view ourselves in it, as in a mirror,
for we cannot appreciate its great glory unless we read it with
diligence."

The Book of Psalms is alive with theology. These poems
reveal God at work on behalf of His people: the God of history;
the God of nature; the God of salvation; yes, the God and Father
of our Lord Jesus Christ. To treat all psalms alike, or to handle
them as you would Romans 4 or Colossians 2, is to rob them of
their distinctive beauty and power.

1. Give yourself time.

It seems so easy to select eight or ten "familiar psalms"
and then, week by week, study them and prepare sermons; but
such is not the case. A "familiar psalm" is usually more complex
than we realize. Select the psalms that speak to your own heart
and that seem to meet your own needs. Or select psalms that
are favorites in your congregation. Read them repeatedly, and
meditate on them, until their message comes through to you.
Read them in different versions so you can be liberated from
familiar phrases that may hide new truths.

2. Major on the practical.

Where does the experience of the psalmist touch life today?
The setting of the psalm may be different from that of a modern
congregation, but the problems and feelings are the same. Use
your sanctified imagination, and try to penetrate the heart and
mind of the writer. The imagery and symbolism of the Psalms

are a challenge and a delight to the dedicated expositor. Symbols speak to every age. They reveal how contemporary these poems really are.

3. Come to grips with theology.

What does the psalm teach about God, man, sin, redemption, faith, the Word, the church, the future? "The Psalter is a book for the greatest and holiest theologians," said Luther. When Spurgeon was writing his monumental *Treasury of David*, he said that the Book of Psalms "is a bush burning with fire and not consumed." It behooves the expositor to take off his shoes, for he is on holy ground.

4. Study the setting.

Putting the poem into its historical context will help you understand it better and apply it to life today. Some of the settings may elude us, but let's do our best. Maclaren's classic volume, *The Life of David as Reflected in His Psalms*, is helpful here. The book is out of print, but you never know when a copy might appear. Watch!

5. Use your New Testament.

Follow the cross references in a good study Bible, and see what the New Testament has to say about the text. Without resorting to extreme typology, look for Christ in the Psalms. Look for the common experiences of His old covenant and new covenant people and also for the common promises that we can claim. Remember that the Book of Psalms was the hymnal of the New Testament church.

6. Outline carefully.

This means permitting the development of the message to follow the natural contours of the psalm. Avoid forcing some artificial outline on the text. (Of course, we should follow this principle with every passage we preach, not just with the psalms.) While you need not preach everything in the psalm, you must take everything into consideration as you interpret. These songs gushed out from hearts seeking after God, so don't expect them always to outline in a neat and tidy way.

Let your outlines be interpretive and not descriptive. An outline such as "David's trial," "David's trust" and "David's triumph" may be "preachable," but it could be used for any number of different psalms. Furthermore, it is in the past tense—what happened to David—and effective preaching should be in the present tense.

No matter how similar different psalms may appear to be, each one still has its distinctive message. Look for that distinctive, and build on it.

7. Use your imagination.

I am not encouraging fancy, but imagination. Fancy helps you *escape* reality, while imagination helps you *penetrate* reality and understand it better. When the psalmist writes about hills and mountains skipping like rams (Psalm 114), it is time to start using your imagination.

Eugene Peterson does an excellent job of preaching the Psalms. Get his two books *A Long Obedience in the Same Direction* and *Earth and Altar*, both published by InterVarsity Press. You should also study the sermons of Alexander Maclaren (Baker Book House) to see how this master expositor dealt with the Psalms. He prepared from the original Hebrew and was a careful student. You might also want to look at my book *Meet Yourself in the Psalms* (Victor).

Those who love outlines, especially alliterated outlines, will enjoy *Exploring the Psalms* by John Phillips (Loizeaux). Phillips is an excellent preacher, and his volumes are filled with meaty material. Just don't try to imitate his approach. It comes naturally to him, but it may be very artificial if you use it.

The volume on the Psalms in W. Graham Scroggie's *Know Your Bible* series is very good (Revell). Scroggie can get you started in the right direction. A.G. Clarke's *Analytical Studies in the Psalms* (Kregel) is also useful. Again, beware of imitating this alliterative approach.

The Symbolism of the Biblical World by Othmar Keel (Seabury) is a must for the careful expositor who wants information to assist his imagination in interpretation. Keep this volume near at hand; you will use it often.

C.S. Lewis's *Reflections on the Psalms* (Harcourt Brace Jovanovich) is a book to read before you start your series. You should also refer often to *A Christian Handbook to the Psalms* by R.E.O. White (Eerdmans). Be sure to read the introduction first.

A most helpful tool is *The Old Testament Books of Poetry From 26 Translations*, edited by Curtis Vaughan (Zondervan). But please don't drown your people with quotes from a dozen translations in each message.

My favorite commentary on the Psalms is by A.F. Kirkpatrick in the old Cambridge Bible. It has been reprinted by Baker Book House and also by Scripture Truth. Number two on my list is Maclaren in the *Expositor's Bible*. Derek Kidner's two volumes in the Tyndale Old Testament series (IVP) are concise but rich, and I would not want to be without them.

Thirsting for God, by C. Donald Cole (Crossway) is a delightful study on the Psalms from both a devotional and historical point of view. Dr. Cole is one of my favorite radio speakers; his ministry is biblical and practical—and courageous.

All of the standard commentaries have something to contribute, and each of us has his favorites. Lange is especially good in the Psalms, and don't ignore some of the better one-volume commentaries for that quick overview of each psalm.

I am not as excited about Spurgeon's *Treasury of David* as some of my friends are, mainly because the approach is textual. However, you should have the set in your library; it will give you helpful hints along the way.

Preaching from the Psalms can be a spiritual and intellectual challenge for the preacher as well as a test of his pastoral sensitivity. The Psalms grow on you.

"The delightful study on the Psalms has yielded me boundless profit and ever-growing pleasure," said Spurgeon. I can say a hearty "Amen!" to that testimony from my own limited experience. I trust it will be your testimony as well.

32

Anticipating Advent

N ow is the time for all dedicated preachers to start preparing
for the Christmas season. There are four Sundays in the
Advent season, and if you wanted to do a series of five
messages, you could include the Sunday after Christmas
for a total of five.

Why preach a Christmas series? Because people are
thinking about the season, for one thing: and wise is the minister
who sows his seed when the soil is ready. We do not emphasize
the miracle of the Incarnation as we should, or else we deal with
it in a cursory manner.

We keep recommending that you give a series of messages
during the four Sundays of Advent, and our mail indicates that
some of you are taking the suggestion and having a great time.

The danger is that we try to dream up something new for
the Christmas season and we end up with novelty instead of
creativity. For the most part, our people want "the old, old
story." We may have nothing new to say, but we do want to say
it in a new and more meaningful way.

Luke 2:1-10 suggests a series on "The First Christmas."
You have here:

1) The First Christmas Gift, vv. 1-7;
2) The First Christmas Greeting, vv. 8-12;
3) The First Christmas Carol, vv. 13-14; and
4) The First Christmas Rush, vv. 15-20.

For some reason, the Micah 5:2 prophecy has been neglected; and yet it can be approached topically to describe the meaning of Christmas:

1) Where He came from—eternity;
2) Where He came to—Bethlehem;
3) What He came for—to rule;
4) What our response should be—go to Him by faith (Matt. 2:1-12).

You can cram a great deal of solid doctrine into a series like this!

Dr. Luke's record of Mary's varied experiences is rich with material for a series centered about the mother of our Lord (Luke 1:43). Her song in Luke 2:46-55 reveals that God is mindful of us (vv. 46-49), mighty for us (vv. 50-53) and merciful to us (vv. 54, 55).

Use your concordance and locate all the "Christmas beatitudes," the verses that contain "blessed." At the same time, note the many references to joy. Surely they ought to point the way to a Merry Christmas!

However, not everybody is joyful at this special season. There are some who have broken hearts for one reason or another, so keep them in mind as you prepare your messages. Remember the weeping parents of the slain children (Matt. 2:16-18) and the prophecy of Mary's sorrow (Luke 2:35).

Tremendous truths

"The Word became flesh. . . . " What a tremendous truth! You can develop a series around the names of our Lord found in Isaiah 9:6. If you make the first name "Wonderful Counselor," you will have four messages; follow the KJV and some other versions, and you will have five. You can close the series after Christmas if you decide to preach on five names.

For an example of a series on Isaiah 9:6, see my little book *His Name Is Wonderful* (Tyndale).

Another helpful series can be based on the word "manifest" in 1 John. Why was Christ manifested in flesh? That He might reveal eternal life (1:1-4); that He might take away sin (3:5); that He might defeat Satan (3:8); and that He might reveal God's love (4:9).

"The Songs of Christmas" would make an interesting Advent series. You will want to use the songs of Mary (Luke 1:46-56), Zacharias (Luke 1:67-80), the angels (Luke 2:8-14) and Simeon (Luke 2:25-35).

The glory of God

The "glory of God" is a key topic in the story of the Incarnation (John 1:14). Perhaps you could trace the glory of God in the Scriptures—in the tabernacle and temple, in the Person of Jesus Christ, in the church and in the individual believer. Get your concordances out and study the glory of God! Note especially how Ezekiel describes the departing of the glory from the temple.

Along with the word "glory," there are other words that are important in the Christmas story; joy (Luke 2:10), peace (Luke 2:14) and grace (2 Cor. 8:9) come to mind.

Christmas questions

I once did a series on four "Christmas Questions": (1) Why Bethlehem? (2) Why Shepherds? (3) Why a Baby? (4) Why the Magi?

You might consider four messages on "The Savior's Birth

Announcements." Begin with the Old Testament announcements, starting, of course, with Genesis 3:15. But don't just string together a series of prophecies—build the texts into practical messages that encourage the heart.

Continue with the announcement of the angels, and then the announcements of the star. You could use Hebrews 10 for the last message—the Savior's own birth announcement: "Lo, I come!"

Christmas preaching demands imagination, but the rewards are worth all the praying, studying and planning that you do. The prepared preacher can, with God's help, penetrate that "commercial complex" that too often clouds the minds of people at the Christmas season.

33

Advice from the Masters

While strolling among my books, I suddenly got the idea of asking some of the master preachers for counsel that would help me become a better preacher of God's Word. They were ready and eager!

"To set one's heart on being popular is fatal to the preacher's best growth," said Phillips Brooks. "It is the worst and feeblest part of your congregation that makes itself heard in vociferous applause, and it applauds that in you which pleases it. . . . To be your own best self for your people's sake—that is the true law of the minister's devotion."

"Let your own personality, with its distinct point of view and its distinct characteristics, have its natural elbowroom," said James Black. "Borrowed beliefs have no power."

The chief end of preaching

"Preaching . . . is a transaction between the preacher and the listener," added Dr. D. Martyn Lloyd-Jones. "It does

141

something for the soul of man, for the whole of the person, the entire man; it deals with him in a vital and radical manner....What is the chief end of preaching? It is to give to men and women a sense of God and His presence."

So far, so good. But others on my shelves are asking for their turn to share. Yes, Dr. John Henry Jowett?

The sense of wonder

"If we lose the sense of the wonder of our commission, we shall become like common traders in a common market, babbling about common wares. . . . This sense of great personal surprise in the glory of our vocation, while it will keep us humble, will also make us great. It will save us from becoming small officials in transient enterprises. It will make us truly big, and will, therefore, save us from spending days in trifling."

A good word, Dr. Jowett. I see that one of your predecessors, Dr. G. Campbell Morgan, has something to share with us. Dr. Morgan:

"I think we are making a great mistake in much of our thinking and training when we imagine that every Christian minister ought to be somewhat of a prophet, somewhat of an evangelist, and somewhat of a pastor and teacher. I believe that today in the Christian Church these gifts are entirely distinct. But preaching is the vocation of all of them. . . . The supreme work of the Christian minister is the work of preaching."

Thank you, Dr. Morgan. Could you, before you go, give us your personal definition of preaching?

The grace of God

"Preaching is the declaration of the grace of God to human need on the authority of the Throne of God; and it demands on the part of those who hear that they show obedience to the thing declared."

I notice the "father" of American homiletical teaching anxious to say something. Dr. John A. Broadus, the floor is yours:

"After all our preparation, general and special, for the conduct of public worship and for preaching, our dependence for real success is on the Spirit of God. And where one preaches the Gospel, in reliance on God's blessing, he never preaches in vain.

"Nor must we forget the power of character and life to reinforce speech. What a preacher *is*, goes far to determine the effect of what he *says*. There is a medieval proverb, 'If a man's life be lightning, his words are thunders.'"

Great words with little meaning

Dr. A. J. Gossip has a word for us:

"If you are not to drift into unconscious hypocrisy, or at least into using great words with little meaning, always a dangerous thing, live close to Jesus Christ.

"The mass of trouble in a congregation is quite unbelievable. And they come up to church, looking to you to help them, hoping for some word that will bring them through."

Sorry, gentlemen, but our time is just about up. Oh, I'm very sorry, Mr. Spurgeon! I didn't see you get off the shelf. We'll give you the privilege of having the last word:

A fire within

"We believe in waiting, weeping, and agonizing; we believe in a non-success which prepares us for doing greater and higher work, for which we should not have been fitted unless anguish had sharpened our soul.

"I thank God that I can say this—there is no member of my church, no officer of the church, and no man in the world, to whom I am afraid to say before his face what I would say behind his back. Under God, I owe my position in my own church to the absence of all policy, and the habit of always saying what I mean. The plan of making things pleasant all round is a perilous as well as a wicked one.

"I preach—I dare to say it—because I can do no otherwise; I cannot refrain myself; a fire burns within my bones which will consume me if I hold my peace.

"Preach the gospel very decidedly and firmly, no matter what people may say of you, and God will be with you."

Lights out! Good night, brethren!